There Ain't No Gentle Cycle on the Washing Machine of Love

For Ed —

Great friend and a
great General — not a
mentor. Auburn fan.
    Stay well

        Alex

Alex McRae

ISBN # 978-1973830733

Table of Contents

Why I wrote this book

On a slow day in the early '90s I had some extra time on my hands and a dinosaur of a word processor that was gathering dust on the table. I decided to use it.

I already knew I could write a little. I'd sold thousands of words to advertising agencies and businesses and still had a copy of my first composition, a fifth grade science report titled "The Sly Ol' Fox." (I found it in my mother's belongings when she graduated to Heaven. I kept it for some reason.)

I sat down and wrote something I thought resembled a newspaper column. It was supposed to be funny. I was so proud of it, I submitted it under a false name.

My friends at the *Newnan Times-Herald* had the guts to publish it. Some readers liked it, and I was invited to write some more columns. Two years later, I came out of the literary closet and started writing under my real name and working full time for the *Times-Herald*.

I wrote about things I liked and didn't, things I understood and didn't, things I saw and people that interested me. The columns made some people happy and left others outraged, so I figured I was doing something right.

One day, I took one of my frequent trips to Scott's Book Store in downtown Newnan. The store's owner and namesake, Earlene Scott, caught me browsing the low-rent thrillers and said, "You ought to write a book. I think you could sell some."

If you never made it to Scott's, you missed a treat. The store is closed now, but back then, it was one of the great independent bookstores in America.

Earlene either had a copy of every book you'd want to read or was ready to order it for you and call you when your book came in.

Big-name authors were always showing up to sign books, and little-knowns were invited to do the same and received the same first-class treatment. If you were a writer, Earlene nurtured you as if you had some talent, whether you did or not.

When she told me I ought to write a book, I didn't think she meant literary stardom was waiting in the wings. Earlene didn't *guarantee* me a single sale. I didn't know if I had the talent or willpower to do the job, but I decided a book was worth a try.

Twenty-three years later, I finally got around to it.

It's hard to sort through over 2,000 columns and pick a hundred or so you think people might like, but I did the best I could.

I tried to include columns that would please—or offend—just about anybody. If I missed your sweet spot, sorry.

Included here are stories about sex, drugs, rock & roll, religion, romance, armadillos, cats, and the joys and horrors of parenthood. Maybe a touch of politics.

Most people can't tolerate a large dose of me, but some can.

One of them is Earlene Scott. No one ever loved books and writers—even bad ones—more. If you like this book, thank her. If you don't, blame me.

Prologue

Thanks are in order to everyone I came across, read or heard about that gave me an idea for one of these columns.

Some of them were total strangers. Some of them were dear to my heart. Many still are.

In the interest of avoiding legal action, I have changed the names of anyone mentioned in columns featuring me and the people I rubbed up against over the years. If your real name is in this book, I figured you were man—or woman—enough to take it. Deal with it.

Once I started pulling the old columns out, I was struck by how much my writing had changed over the years. And my attitude.

The writing is much tighter these days. So is my lifestyle. I've never been the poster boy for good behavior, but I'm getting better. Sometimes, I'm almost good.

Most of these columns were written between 1995 and 2005. When I started writing, I still cussed a little. That's reflected in these stories. I'm mildly proud that the few profanities included here aren't anything you didn't read in *Gone With the Wind*.

The real credit for putting this thing together and tolerating my whining, whims and delays goes to my wife, Angela.

She's my love and my pal and my best buddy and favorite traveling companion. She's also a great writer and editor. Other than Christmas decorations and Oxford commas, we agree on most things.

Cover Art

The cover for this book was created by my great friend David Boyd Sr. I have to include the "Sr." because his son, David Jr., is an outstanding artist in his own right.

If you don't know David Boyd, you've missed a treat. In addition to spending decades as an award-winning political cartoonist and cranking out thousands of comic strips for newspapers across the nation, Boyd has produced countless caricatures of famous and infamous people—including me. He did some sculpture, too, and it isn't awful at all. His work is displayed in the finest museums, businesses and trailer parks of America.

Boyd may be best known for the illustrations he provided for two American icons—Lewis Grizzard and Jeff Foxworthy.

For my money, Grizzard is the best columnist that ever lived. He and Boyd became good friends, and Boyd still reminisces about Lewis's golf game and romantic habits.

If you don't know who Jeff Foxworthy is, you might *not* be a redneck. Foxworthy's recordings are the best-selling comedy albums (CDs, downloads, etc.) in history. He is equally notorious for his series of "You Might be a Redneck" books. The covers and inside illustrations for many of Foxworthy's books, calendars, T-shirts, greeting cards and place mats are David Boyd's work.

Boyd's a legend. I'm honored he agreed to do the cover for this book. Plus, the price was right. Don't try to figure out the deep symbolism on the cover illustration. I don't understand it, either. I just know it's good.

The only question I asked Boyd was, "Why did you stick a chicken on my book cover?"

He said the chicken was symbolic of every low-rent person in America, and I fit the bill perfectly. I couldn't have been prouder.

I've never had a better friend, and you've never seen a better artist.

GROWING UP

Everyone thinks their childhood was unique.

I'm no exception. But childhoods go in different directions.

Here's a piece of my journey. It explains a lot, I think.

I Get Around

Ricky Robbins had red hair, a blue Ford and the thinnest lips I'd ever seen. I figured he'd worn them out playing all those high notes on the trumpet. Ricky said it was wear and tear from all the girls he'd kissed, but I didn't believe it for a minute. I knew enough Baptist philosophy to be absolutely certain that any 18-year-old with that many notches on his lips would have gone to hell prematurely for overindulging in one of God's most precious gifts.

Ricky's pride and joy was a '56 Ford with a dazzling paint job, four-speed Hurst shifter and a high-performance heater.

We played in the high school dance band, one of those with saxophones and trumpets and trombones. We wore plaid tuxedo jackets and weren't sexy rock and rollers but still did a steady business, especially at winter and spring "dress-up" dances.

One Friday night we were playing a Valentine's dance at a small south Alabama town when a winter storm moved in ahead of schedule. The storm was a monster, and as the evening wore on you could feel winter's grip closing tight around the school gym. By the time we played "Good Night, Ladies," temperatures were in the teens and dropping fast.

With three others, I had ridden to the dance in our bass player's station wagon. The heat in the wagon had been balky earlier and had now expired completely. The four of us searched for blankets and braced ourselves for a cold drive.

But Ricky had driven down by himself, and while his backseat was full of junk, the shotgun spot was available for the ride home. We drew straws for the honor, and I won.

That heater was amazing. In moments I felt like one of those biblical dudes in the fiery furnace. Things got even hotter when Ricky began spinning lurid tales about his backseat exploits, which, if true, would have tested even an Olympic-caliber gymnast.

I took it all in with a grain of salt and a blast of hot air, but as we rode north, I made an observation. At every small town we passed through, an interesting phenomenon occurred. Ricky would stop at the main intersection and gun his engine until the ground shook and the straight pipes threatened to melt. If there was a girl in sight, she looked. Always. And the look definitely did *not* say "bug off."

When we got home, Ricky dropped me off in the school parking lot, and I piled into my 1960 Ford Falcon for the trip home. On the way, I stopped at an all-night Krystal.

When I drove up, the joint was almost empty. Halfway through my second glass of milk and an extra side of bacon, she came in and took a seat just down the counter. Sultry, salacious and sensual, she was definitely a bad girl. And she was all by herself. Just like me.

I put on my best James Dean and looked her way. She looked back with a vaguely nauseated expression. She didn't look up again, but by the time I finished eating and started walking to the car, I had a plan that I knew would get her attention.

I still had one ace to play. My car didn't have rolled and pleated interior or a competition engine like Ricky's, but it had tires. And I knew how to make them sing.

I shoved in the clutch, fired that puny engine and started turning some serious RPMs. When the engine threatened to explode, I popped the clutch and held on tight as the world became a blur.

The tires spun and whirled and shrieked. The air was thick with smoke and the stench of burning rubber as I shot off like a rocket. Straight backwards. Right into a telephone pole.

In my excitement, I had left the car in reverse. It cost me about 200 bucks to fix that car, but it was worth every penny.

Because for one unforgettably perfect moment, that gorgeous girl had looked. Looked right at me. I believe it was just before she started laughing so hard the milk spewed out her nose.

I got the look, but I learned a lesson. Fast cars or slow, it doesn't matter. You won't get far with a girl as long as you're stuck in reverse.

The Ultimate Career Burnout

Mom and Pop must have figured out early I wasn't exactly "mainstream" material. They must have known my attitude and temperament would lead to some problems as I grew up. Problems like finding a job.

So every time I got excited about anything, the folks encouraged the endeavor, hoping it might lead to something down the road. The process started when I became enchanted with the comic book character Prince Valiant. I came home one day to find a complete Prince Valiant outfit laid out on the couch. It was fabulous: a Viking-style helmet, shield emblazoned with the trademark horse's head and, best of all, a really cool plastic sword.

For a few months I spent hours holding imaginary sword fights with fearsome enemies and slaying any crawfish brave enough to crawl out of the creek behind the house. I rescued imaginary damsels, fought off pagan armies and saved the world on a daily basis.

After I heard about Harry Houdini, I ditched Prince Valiant in favor of becoming the world's greatest magician. Soon, a magician's "starter kit" appeared.

There was one problem. Doing illusions takes lots of patience and lots of practice. I didn't have the former and didn't do the latter and the result was predictable. At my first and only public appearance I was a total flop. I ran home, took the Prince Valiant outfit out of mothballs and killed my magic set.

Other flirtations followed, and Mom and Pop couldn't have been more supportive. But their indulgence had limits. And those limits were on display at an amusement park on the shores of Lake Pontchartrain, just up the street from where we lived in New Orleans.

The big wooden roller coaster was eye-popping and the midway shows and carnival rides were a young kid's paradise. At one time or another I wanted to be like every performer I saw. Mother laughed at my efforts to duplicate the loose-jointed feats of the contortionist billed as "Plastic Man." She tolerated my attempts to juggle the household oranges, but knowing the Prince Valiant gear was still in the closet, when she saw me eyeing the sword-swallower with interest, she said, "Don't even think about it."

The performer that fascinated me most, though, was the guy in the gun, a certified human cannonball who was billed as something that sounded like "The Great Zucchini."

Countless times I watched as the man stood at the throat of a huge cannon with his white cape fluttering in the humid breeze. Then he'd smile and wave and disappear into the weapon's depths.

Seconds later, with a giant roar and huge puff of smoke, the Great Zucchini came sailing out of the cannon and soared for what seemed like miles before he landed in a net, popped up and waved to the adoring crowd.

It looked like the coolest job ever. But today I'm glad I didn't pursue it. I might have wound up like Brian Miser, who is the human cannonball for the Barnum & Bailey Circus. Miser has over 800 flights to his credit, but right now he's out of work after the City of Grand Rapids, Michigan, refused to let him perform during the Barnum & Bailey Circus's Grand Rapids stop.

Officials don't object to Miser acting like a missile. It's the other thing. To add a little excitement to the spectacle, Miser's wife douses him with lighter fluid and ignites him before each launch. The result has earned Miser the nickname "Bailey's Comet."

Except in Grand Rapids. Officials said setting a man on fire wasn't setting a good example for local kids. Especially during Fire Prevention Week.

They're probably right. And I'm sure Miser's career will flourish in a less fire-conscious venue. It just goes to show that even a dream job has its drawbacks. I'll try and remember that—as soon as I find my Prince Valiant outfit.

A Golden Oldie Makes a Comeback

Mid-sixties. College dorm room. Late night. Bored to tears.

Then a far-off murmur swelled to a high-pitched roar as a crowd of coeds passed by on the sidewalk outside my window, chanting and squealing and producing some very unladylike noises.

A friend came bursting through the door, shaking and stammering, barely able to control himself. "Come on!" he said. "We gotta go. I heard somebody say they're gonna burn their bras."

"Get out," I croaked. "They're gonna start a fire? With their bras? It's not that cold outside."

"They're not cold," he said. "They're burning their bras to protest."

"Protest what?" I asked lamely.

"Who cares?" my friend said. "They're taking off their bras. Let's go watch."

And so we did. As protests go, it was a haphazard affair, obviously organized at the last minute, perhaps with the aid of a few bottles of Boone's Farm. The ladies lurched around in a circle, waving arms and undergarments, chanting things like "Equal rights" and "Freedom now."

A few made speeches about abolishing curfews at the girls' dorms so they could stay out all night and party just like the boys did. Since the guys didn't have a curfew, the proposal sounded fair to me.

Someone finally produced a small trash can and a vial of lighter fluid, and several bras were soaked and set afire. As nylon melted and underwires groaned and snapped, several more women slipped undergarments from beneath their frumpy sweatshirts and tossed them onto the pyre.

Eventually, some of the sorority girls showed up and decided to play. It took them a while to get in the swing of things, but after fumbling clumsily through several layers of Bobbie Brooks sportswear, they produced their bras, waved them daintily around a time or two and tossed them into the flames.

The event's organizer was Ms. Hilde Swenson, a Swedish transfer student with an IQ the size of Mount Everest and a cup size to match. Hilde's bra was the last to be removed, and once she was freed from her Maidenform bondage, the crowd of boys couldn't take their eyes off her T-shirt, which heaved ominously as her unfettered flesh rolled and swayed beneath the thin cotton fabric like a migrating herd of fleshy elk. It was magnificent.

The subsequent years were filled with fond memories. On countless occasions I was accosted by bra-less women who walked up, looked me in the eye, and with body parts a-bounce said, "You are a male chauvinist pig. No longer will I submit to your domination. I am free. I am woman. Look at me."

I always did, gladly, and tried not to drool too much.

But eventually, enough civil rights legislation was passed to convince women to put their bras back on and get down to the business of taking over the business world. And all too soon, bra burning was a fond memory.

Until now.

Recently, a group of female workers at a Johnstown, Pennsylvania, plant that manufactures brassieres yanked off their bras and set them on fire in protest. Only this time, they weren't protesting inequality...they were protesting layoffs after the company announced it was cutting 600 jobs due to sagging global bra sales.

I hope the girls had fun and I hope no body parts were bruised, battered or sprained in the protest, but I've got a hard time getting up any sympathy for this one.

These women were burning bras because they're losing jobs, but they're losing jobs because women are buying fewer bras. Which means there must be more and more uppity, independent minded, bra-less women out there. That ought to be good news for all women. But I guess not. I guess right now, the girls at that manufacturing plant must feel that instead of half full, their cups are half empty.

Still Priceless After All These Years

I knew by the sixth grade I would never amount to much in a jockstrap and turned my attention to something I loved better than sports...books. From Nostradamus to Nancy Drew, I read everything I could beg, borrow or steal, and I still do.

I didn't spend as much time reading the Good Book as I should have, but thanks to my mother, I carried one around several days a week and once earned a gold star and a donut in Sunday School for being the first one to memorize the books of the Bible, which made it seem worthwhile at the time.

In junior high, I joined a church boy's group called the Royal Ambassadors. We met weekly and, between devotional poundings, engaged in allegedly fun activities, including one that actually was...the Sword Drill.

During this exercise, several of us stood in the front of a room, holding a set of identical hard-backed Bibles at our sides. The leader of the event would name a chapter and verse from the Bible and say "Go!" and we'd whip those Bibles to attention and start flying through the pages. The first one to find the proper scripture won.

I never lost, thanks to my expertise in one particular Biblical area. Everyone could find Genesis and Revelation, and Psalms was roughly at the center of things, so that was a snap. And the New Testament seemed fairly straightforward to everyone except my friend Ralph, who always confused Galatians and Colossians and once combined the two to invent a new book he called Golossians, which sounded like a tribe of people who wore rubber rain boots.

But it was my skill with the Minor Prophets that always put me over the top. Never once did I confuse Zephaniah with Zechariah, I knew Amos and Obadiah from Amos 'n Andy and never, ever faltered when pursuing those two most elusive books, Nahum and Habakkuk.

But while I never read most of the books I located so easily, I had listened to enough sermons over the years to know Salvation was free. Period. No down payment, no weekly payments, no carrying costs. It was free. To my knowledge, it worked that way for every branch of the Protestant Christian tree...whether sprinkled, immersed or finely misted, no one bought their way into Heaven.

As far as I know, while everything else in the world has changed since my Sword Drill days, the Bible's teachings have not. But apparently, a Utah woman missed the rather basic scriptural lesson about the price of redemption.

According to the Associated Press, Ms. Kaziah Hancock, of the metro Salt Lake City area, recently donated a tract of land to her church, an outfit with the rather long-winded name of the True and Living Church of Jesus Christ of the Saints of the Last Days. In return, the church agreed to keep Hancock's other debts current and—in what was obviously the deal clincher—promised her a chance to meet Christ on earth.

Apparently, a timetable was not given as to when the Lord would arrive to thank Ms. Hancock for her generous donation. After He failed to appear soon enough to suit her, she first got itchy, then downright litigious. Hancock finally sued the church to get her land back. She won and will soon be compensated for her stupidity.

Which is as it should be, but here's my question. Even if some slick-talking preacher was able to convince this woman there was a chance to have high tea with Jesus at the kitchen table, what on earth made her think she could arrange this for $290,000, the price of the donated land?

Sure, $290,000 is a hefty fee, but consider this: the Atlanta Falcons recently sold for $545 million. Given that statement on the value of the dollar, there may not be a supercomputer large enough to calculate what a visit from Jesus would be worth.

The Scent of Love

These days I settle for soap, but when I was young and single I spent a small fortune trying to make myself smell better. Prowling high-priced boutiques and bargain-basement drug stores, I spent endless hours and countless paychecks seeking the holy grail of fragrances, the odor that would make the ladies melt with a single sniff.

For a time I favored something called Canoe. I don't know if they even make it anymore. After reading a particularly steamy James Bond novel, I picked up a sample of the superspy's favorite aroma. Despite the fact that it reeked like a Paris street urinal, I poured it on, figuring if I smelled like Agent 007 I'd have to ice down my mattress to keep it from overheating. Even during periods of budgetary distress I managed to keep myself in Aqua Velva rather than go scentless.

Despite years of such blatant nostril trolling, I spent most of my evenings home alone, a stinky loser in the game of love.

Now I know why. According to Martha McClintock and Suma Jacob, I should have just hosed myself down with tap water and let Mother Nature do the romantic heavy lifting.

McClintock is a psychologist at the University of Chicago. Jacob is her student assistant. For quite a while now, these two have been studying how smells affect a person's mood.

The smell phenomenon is not a new one. Everyone's a sucker for "new car," and most of us gag over "used cat litter." But the Chicago research turned up some rather unexpected results: namely, that a certain substance exists that is a certifiable winner in the dating derby.

It's not Aramis or Polo or Obsession or even Eau de Lube Job. The stuff that has the Chicago girls gushing is androstadienone (say "an-DROS-ta-DIE-en-own"). Let's call it the Big A for short.

The Big A is produced when a man's body breaks down testosterone. Though odorless and colorless, this manly substance is said to move women more profoundly than a truckload of SALE! signs.

In the study, female test subjects had their upper lips swabbed with a mystery substance. Some received the Big A, others a placebo. Immediately following the anointing, the women were asked to keep a journal of their moods as they endured numerous interviews and filled out lengthy questionnaires.

The results were surprising. Those women given the placebo became progressively more cranky and irritable during the post-swab hours. But following an exposure to the Big A, test subjects remained, for hours, in a good mood.

A good mood. Well, it's not nibbled ears or even heavy breathing, but at this point in my life, I'll settle any day for a few hours in the company of a good-mooded woman. In fact, I'd more than settle. I'd jump at the chance.

There's one problem, though: applying the stuff. Even though it has been proven to lift a female's spirits, no well-raised guy is gonna run up to a woman and ask if he can wipe his testosterone leftovers on her upper lip.

Still, there must be a way to get this stuff in the right hands. Or under the right noses. Perhaps it could be put in a spray can and given a spiffy label like Happy Girl. Better yet, it could be added to the water supply. Or the United Nations could seed the world's clouds with Big A and let global bliss rain from the heavens.

Any stuff this good needs to be available now. And cost should not be a consideration. After all, how can you put a price on knowing that after centuries of hostilities, the opposing sides in the Battle of the Sexes may finally be able to wave the white flag, hold hands and sway gently side to side as they sing a chorus of "Give Peace A Chance."

Not a Very Bright Idea

Overall, I'd have to say the fifth grade was a good one for me. I joined the scouts for the first time, collected my first kiss courtesy of June Johnson, and was selected to be one of the kids who raised the American flag in front of Cherokee Elementary every day.

There was, however, one unpleasant experience. I still remember it as the day the lights went out and I came on.

After only a year in the school band program, I had achieved such a degree of proficiency on the clarinet that the music teacher asked me to play at a school assembly. I agreed, practiced extra hard for a few days, and on an otherwise normal Friday morning, showed up ready to rip.

As I waited on stage, the other kids entered the lunchroom and took their seats. Then, as the cafeteria curtains were closed and the lights dimmed, a hush fell over the crowd as I began to play.

I played the only song I knew from memory, a miserable little number called "Glow Worm." It was probably my choice of tunes that convinced the music teacher it would be cool to use a black light effect during the performance.

I had never seen a black light in operation before that day and neither had any of the other kids, and when it was illuminated for the first time, there was a collective "Ooooooohhh" from the stunned audience as I stood there wailing away, my freshly laundered white shirt blazing like a beacon.

Soon, the already strange performance took a turn for the worse. The kindergarten teacher had heard about the black light and wanted in on the act, so as I honked my way through chorus after chorus, a long line of five-year-olds, also attired in glowing white garb, humped their way, inchworm style, across the stage and back several times.

At the end of the performance the students were either too sick or too shocked to applaud, but there was a smattering of cheers from the back of the room. Mostly, I suspect, from the mothers of the fifth grade girls who were hoping that maybe my exposure to the mysterious black light might somehow render me sterile before I was old enough to mate with their daughters.

The point being, I know how painful it can be to be caught in the spotlight, especially if you are the spotlight.

Which is why I'm so upset with the bizarre research work being done by a group of so-called scientists in Oregon.

These test-tube jockeys have succeeded in making a monkey glow in the dark by exposing it to the same chemicals that make jellyfish shine and glow worms glimmer.

Sorry, but you gotta draw the line somewhere. I'm not an animal rights freak. I think sometimes, but only sometimes, it is necessary to use animals for scientific testing. But only for some great and good purpose.

I defy anyone to tell me how the common good is enhanced by making a monkey imitate a fluorescent lightbulb.

I suppose if we had a national power blackout we could line up glowing monkeys along the runways of America's airports and have them serve as emergency landing lights. But somehow, having monkeys as an emergency light source doesn't feel right.

"Dern, Marge, the storm's done knocked the power out. Hand me a candle."

"Ain't got none, Earl. Used the last one lighting that can of Sterno we cooked supper with."

"Well, then, hand me a monkey. I can't see a thing."

This glowing monkey business is totally bogus. Not only is glowing unnecessary, but it is also humiliating. I know from firsthand experience.

I don't know the glowing monkey, but I feel his pain. These dudes in Oregon need to desist immediately. It seems obvious that in this case, what we need isn't brighter monkeys but brighter scientists.

Pumps and Puppies

Hurricane Katrina did a job on my hometown. A lot of New Orleans will never be rebuilt. Millions who lived or visited there over the years will be left with only their memories. That crowd includes me.

In the coming years I'm sure I'll look back on funny stories and happy times. But right now my main memory of New Orleans involves a big pump and a little dog.

My best friend, Danny Sander, lived on Marconi Boulevard. City Park was right across the street. So was a curious-looking structure that wouldn't exist anywhere else.

Anyone watching the coverage of Hurricane Katrina's aftermath has heard about the elaborate system of pumps that is needed to drain water out of New Orleans every time it rains.

One of those pumping stations was across the street from Danny Sander's house. It had two main features: a huge pipe and a small pond that collected floodwater for the pipe to suck up and deposit into the Marconi Boulevard Canal, which took the water out to Lake Pontchartrain.

The pumps didn't operate too often, but the small pond stayed busy. Stupid kids like me took fishing poles over there and tried to catch something in a fully enclosed body of water that would never be home to anything other than a crawfish family.

And the little pond had one more purpose. At least for a guy down the street named Pete.

I'd seen Pete plenty but didn't know his last name. And didn't want to. He was the neighborhood grouch, a gloomy, heavy-bearded bad boy who never had a kind word for anybody.

Pete also had some dogs. I wasn't on speaking terms with any of his mutts and didn't want to be if they were anything like their owner. That changed one afternoon when I was walking home past Pete's house and saw him stuffing live puppies into a burlap sack.

I'd never seen anything like it. And as much as I didn't want to get near Pete, I eased into his driveway and asked what he was doing.

He said his female dog had given birth to another litter. He said he didn't need any puppies, so he was going to throw them into the pumping station pond and drown them.

I was horrified. I was more scared that those puppies would drown than I was of my mother, who would not even talk about having a dog. I begged Pete not to throw the puppies in the pond. When he didn't change his mind, I asked if he would give one to me.

He did, then walked off toward the pumping station. I remember seeing that burlap sack wiggle, hearing the puppies squealing inside.

Mother almost fainted when I showed up with a dog. I was ready for a big fight, but when I told her the situation, she said, "OK, we'll take him in."

At that point he needed a name. I did the honors, and he became Pickles.

He was black and dumb and maybe because he had come so close to death, he was overflowing with life. After Pickles was past his bottle-feeding days, Mother put her foot down and said he had to move outside.

Daddy built a small pen and a doghouse. It rained a lot in New Orleans. Every time it did, Pickles came out of his doghouse and sat on top. My sister and I would watch him through the window and shake our heads.

When it was time to play, you had to open the pen and hide, because he would jump all over you, trying to cover your face with sloppy, wet kisses.

Pickles is long gone. But today when I see the devastation, I think about that big pump. And I think about that little puppy. And I think about a town that will never be the same.

SPORTS AND LEISURE

Except for a brief starring role at first base for the
Dalraida Baptist Church high school softball team,
I stank at sports. But I've always loved to watch,
and I'm a huge fan.

I've seen some great games and suffered some brutal losses.
Luckily, I always knew that fun and games don't
always go hand in hand.

A Girl Can't Be Too Careful

There was a little girl who had a little curl, right in the middle of her forehead. Trouble is, what she needed was a piece of plastic in her pants.

Once again gender equity rears its ugly head. This time, at the ballpark.

This recent turmoil was triggered when 12-year-old Melissa Raglan got the boot from a Boca Raton, Florida, youth league baseball game.

Melissa is a girl. And that's OK. Plenty of those playing Little League ball these days. But Melissa plays catcher. And that's the problem.

It seems that during a recent game, the home plate umpire, showing a tenacious concern for sandlot safety, inquired if Melissa was wearing a protective cup. Melissa doffed her headgear, shook out her flowing mane, informed the dude of her chromosome arrangement and thought the issue settled. But before she could crouch again, the surly, sexist ump tossed her for not wearing the proper safety equipment.

Melissa's reaction? "I thought he was nuts."

I think she's right. I'm all for safety, but I'm a bigger fan of common sense. Have these people lost their minds? One baseball league official, in a display of bedrock-deep stupidity, went so far as to say that where Melissa was concerned, wearing her cup was no different than wearing a catcher's mask.

I have to disagree. Last I heard you can't go blind from catching a one-hopper between the legs.

In case you didn't know, let me explain the particular piece of equipment involved.

Basically, a cup is just a piece of hard plastic that fits in your athletic supporter and covers the area where the male reproductive equipment is housed. The cup is designed to keep males safe from the ravages of bouncing balls.

Young ladies, for obvious anatomical reasons, are not in danger of suffering the same type of injury. While medical experts say that even female athletes need a certain amount of groin protection, they think maybe the league went too far.

This position was stated by no less an authority than Coral Gables, Florida, physician Dr. Ramon Iglesias (no relation to crooner Julio), who firmly announced, "There's no medical reason why a woman should wear a jockstrap or a cup."

Certainly no fashion urgency, either, at least until Madonna shows up wearing a jeweled jock at the premiere of her next video. Nevertheless, the league stuck to its guns, banning Melissa to outfield duty until she agreed to buttress her britches boy-style when she's behind the plate.

This is ludicrous. Asking a little girl to wear a cup is like asking a buzzard to wear a parachute. Namely, stupid and unnecessary.

It was a story destined for a sad ending. A crotch-related nightmare on the field of dreams. A blight on the national pastime...

Until help arrived. From, of all places, the Great Smoky Mountains.

The Bike Athletic Company of Knoxville, Tennessee, heard about this young lady's unprotected privates and, in a dramatic display of compassion and savvy marketing, overnighted the solution direct to Boca.

Thanks to the work of these hill-country athletic supporters, young Melissa is back in the ball game, squatting behind home plate, wearing a piece of gear designed especially for young ladies who wish to assume this position.

It's really nothing but a set of padded drawers, but who cares? The beefed-up bloomers fill the bill and satisfy all league safety rules.

It's a potential tragedy that turned out pretty well after all. The league is happy, Melissa gets to catch again, and best of all, she has all the groin protection she needs.

At least until she starts to date.

Pigs and Birdies Duke it Out

Two Southern passions are about to slug it out in the courts as barbeque and birdies square off in Stuart, Florida. OK, so it's really a fight between hogs and golf, but the locals claim it's really a battle between art and culture.

Since "art" and "culture" are vague concepts, let's redefine those terms in light of the Florida fracas. In this case, "art" is country music and "culture" is what the residents of the cleverly named Florida Golf Course hoped to attain when they took delivery of their golf front digs.

Well, why can't the two coexist? Sure, some country clubs have reputations as snooty, top-of-the-heap kinds of places, but these days, country music isn't just confined to trailer parks. At even the loftiest levels of society, Grand Ole and Metropolitan mingle delightfully, opera-wise.

So what's the problem, you ask? Why can't George Jones and golf get along?

Well, maybe they could if the old Possum weren't being played too loud. At least it's too loud for golf course residents Jean and Alice Krentz, who last week filed suit against Paul Thompson, who lives across the fairway from the Krentzes and likes his country music loud.

Well, to be honest, it's not Thompson who likes it loud. It's his herd of 200 hogs. Thompson says the strains of Alan Jackson, Merle Haggard and other country crooners make his hogs happy. He says the music "soothes" the pigs, presumably making them better bacon-makers, if not neighbors.

Of course, Thompson's herd tends to wander, so he has to really crank up his outdoor speakers to make sure every boar and shoat gets an earful of Faith Hill or Shania Twain when Thompson fires it their way.

Understandably, the locals are a little fed up. I can sympathize. I like all kinds of music but always try to keep my personal volume dial hovering somewhere below Book of Revelation level.

In their lawsuit, the Krentzes claim the cacophony has caused a decline in their property values. They contend that the loud music disrupts golfers and turns off prospective homeowners.

I can see their point, but here's my question: Sure, the music is a nuisance, but don't the golfers mind the hogs just as much? I only play golf about once every five years, but I know you don't want some 600-pound

Hampshire hog doing the Boot Scootin' Boogie across the number 6 green when you're trying to sink a three-footer worth a week's pay. Imagine your twosome resorting to this...

"Gol-dern, Ernie. Is that a hog?"

"Looks like it to me."

"Poland China?"

"Durned if I know, Russell, but it's big."

"Shore is. That hog bother you, Ernie?"

"Not really, especially with the wind blowing out. Ain't much smell that way. No, it ain't the hog that's got me down, Russell. It's that music. I'd rather hear a sow bleat 'Dixie' than Conway Twitty mumble 'Hello, Darlin' one more time."

Since the county has no anti-noise ordinance, the law, at least for now, seems to be on the side of hog man Thompson. And even if the hog-hating golfers go forward legally, Thompson vows to stay in the fight. "What we've got is a rich developer trying to use the court system to squeeze out the poor people," he says. "And I'm not squeezing."

So for now, on the lush green fairways of the Florida Golf Course, the Krentzes and other linksters will be teeing off to the groans of Johnny Paycheck, dodging boars in search of birdies and gathering bogies to the tune of "Achy Breaky Heart."

I know the golfers just want a little peace and quiet, but they'd better be careful. It's risky business to come between a man and his sows. Especially when one of them is named Wynonna.

Sports Abroad

Billy Shakespeare once penned a nifty line about something being "full of sound and fury, signifying nothing." He was obviously referring to British sporting events.

I didn't expect to find NASCAR on TV during my recent British excursion, but I hoped I might catch a glimpse of America's Big Three: football, basketball or baseball. Instead I was treated to a steady diet of the Unholy Trinity: rugby, cricket and soccer.

All three are hideous. Rugby is like junior high sandlot football, with people getting in big piles and pushing each other around. Hardly worth a mention. We'll discuss cricket later.

Soccer is the big game Over There. The British call it football, but anyone who knows a jockstrap from a tea cozy can tell you there's a vast difference between the British version and the Real Thing.

In American football, most of the violence takes place on the field. In British football, most of the violence occurs in the stands. I think this violence may be precipitated by the fact that the game itself is an utter bore. To compensate, British fans get roaring drunk and proceed to act like a bunch of recently released convicts at a strip club.

One Sunday I stood in Piccadilly Circus and watched as two groups of drunken fans—separated by flak-jacketed bobbies, steel barriers and eight lanes of asphalt—roared team chants and threw beer cans at each other. It was noon. They were waiting for buses to the stadium, where things would deteriorate even further.

And deteriorate they do. Soccer is the only sport in the UK where police statistics are reported. On the same day I observed the above-described pregame ritual, a newspaper called the *Independent* released a report on which teams led the league the previous year in number of fans arrested.

While Sunderland took top honors with 223 jailings, Chelsea managed a respectable second place with 188 incarcerations, including an absolutely spectacular mass arrest of 100 fans who were locked up after the cops noticed they were carrying weapons (including a meat cleaver) and a bottle of ammonia they intended to douse rival fans with.

Cricket, on the other hand, is rarely fatal. At least for the players. Unlike their soccer counterparts, cricket fans don't chant and scream or throw things at cricket matches. What they really do, I think, is prepare to die. A cricket match makes shuffleboard look like professional wrestling. Soccer teams are mostly sponsored by beer makers and auto parts dealers. Cricket squads should be sponsored by funeral homes.

During a cricket match, a crowd of boring people sit quietly and watch a group of somewhat younger men stand around and attempt to outlive them. The "sport" itself is somewhat like baseball but without any pretense at athleticism.

While the "batsman," padded like a hockey goalie, stands around and guards a set of sticks called a "wicket," the opposing pitcher (or bowler) makes a fifty-yard dash towards the batter, then pulls up and fires the ball with all his might ... straight into the ground. (Yes, the bowler is required to bounce the ball toward the batter.)

At cricket matches, they don't break for halftime. They break for lunch, at which time those spectators without the strength to down a cucumber sandwich swallow a hit of NoDoz and have their vital signs checked while a fleet of hearses idle quietly (and hopefully) nearby.

The hearses always arrive with full fuel tanks. Some matches can last up to FIVE DAYS!

Sorry, but when it comes to sport, give me American. Before some of the British contests, a band struck up "God Save The Queen." Whenever I heard it, all I could think was, "How 'Bout Them Dogs?"

Adventure on the Road

It's one of life's cruel ironies that just when you want something worst, it's suddenly out of reach. Which is where I find myself right now. Since it doesn't look like I'll be taking one soon, all I can think about is vacations.

But since I can't go, I decided to dream one up...the perfect vacation. And I don't mean Disney World at the height of rug rat season. The last time I went to Mickeyville, I had to rest for three days to get up the strength to go back to work.

I figure a fantasy vacation is just the ticket since you can go anywhere in the world for as long as you want and never worry about losing your wallet or being attacked by a terrorist or getting diarrhea from eating foreign food.

My fantasy vacation would include a sip of romance here, a dollop of culture there, and a huge nap whenever the urge struck.

Even though I was making this vacation up, I decided I could still benefit from some expert advice and spent a few evenings checking out the Travel Channel. I was looking for inspiration. What I saw was a horror show.

My dream vacation would include tropical breezes and umbrella-sprouting drinks. Maybe a peaceful mountain stroll or an evening at the dirt track with the guys. But according to the TV travel experts, "normal" vacations are severely out of style.

These days, "theme" vacations are all the rage. And the themes are pretty ugly. One is ecology, which is fine for a stint in the classroom, but nothing to base a vacation on. Apparently eco-vacationers can't find enough ecology in the backyard, so they jet off to some remote jungle and spend days exposing themselves to venomous insects, man-eating fish and man-eating people. The sunset campfire chats are disturbing...

"Oooh, look up there, Lulu. It's a left-handed Afghan Howler Gerbil. When I was back at Wellesley doing my thesis on the Rise of Feminism in Rural Mississippi Honky-tonks, I never dreamed I'd get so close to one."

"Me, neither, Buffy. In fact, last night that little Howler crawled in the sack with me."

"Oooh, whatever did you do?"

"Take these binoculars and see for yourself."

"Is that a hickey on that Howler? You bad girl."

These eco-vacations are mostly taken by ugly women with a fondness for armpit hair and an obvious aversion to makeup of any kind. To be fair, the guys aren't much better, a bunch of undernourished weenies who enjoy sitting around the campfire, talking about their sensitivity training when they're not chirping the more obscure verses of "Kumbaya."

The only thing worse than an eco-vacation is something called an "Adventure Vacation," a brand of leisure obviously designed by the Marquis de Sade. On adventure vacations, people pay big money to get hauled off and dumped in the middle of nowhere with a small pack of food and an extra jockstrap.

They climb mountains, run rapids and hike across deserts with one goal in mind...to survive. And the greater the pain, the more they seem to like it...

"Wow! This blister's the size of a mango. I'm gonna pop it and watch the pus ooze out."

"Yeah, that blister's cool, but check out my ankle."

"Oh, man, it's all red and swollen. Did you sprain it?"

"Nope, it's a bite."

"What kind? Scorpion? Snake, maybe?"

"No, it was a left-handed Afghan Howler Gerbil with a strange injury on its neck. Looked like a hickey, actually. Tomorrow I'll kill it and we can eat it raw."

"Cool."

Sorry, but that's just not for me. In my dream vacation, there are no bugs and no bites and the only time I break a sweat is when I raise my hand. Just long enough to get a waiter's attention as I say, "Another Mai Tai, please. And don't forget the umbrella."

Bad News in Bass Land

A few years ago I did a story about an endangered old building in a nearby small town. I drove out there three or four days in a row, always taking the same route at about the same time of day and seeing the same man doing the same thing.

He sat on the side of the road where a large swampy area had formed near a culvert. He didn't move except to pull in his cane pole to see if he had lost his bait. One day I decided to stop.

I walked up and he asked if he could help me.

I shook my head, introduced myself and said, "I've seen you out here the last few days. You must really like to fish."

"Not that much," he replied.

"Well, then," I asked, "how come you're out here every day if you don't like to fish?"

"I like to eat," he said.

Of course, I thought. Best reason of all to fish. In fact, until not long ago, it was just about the only reason people fished. Other than the so-called "sportsmen" who chased huge marlin or sailfish for the thrill of killing something bigger than them, a man with a fishing pole in his hand was hunting for groceries.

That changed in the mid-sixties when some people in Montgomery, Alabama, got together and formed the Bass Anglers Sportsman Society, or B.A.S.S. It was dedicated to catching largemouth bass, but with a twist. Instead of eating the bass, people were encouraged to throw them back, a practice that came to be known as "Catch and Release."

First time I heard people were throwing back bass, it made perfect sense. When it came to eating, bass were always on the bottom of the menu. For fine food, bream and catfish were the way to go.

They were not only tastier but easier to prepare. With a bream or a catfish, all you had to do was skin or scale it, clean it, gut it and pop it in some hot grease until golden brown. Bass have to be filleted, which is never worth the effort, taste-wise.

But if eating bass never took off, catching them sure did. And then the trouble started.

These days, whether it's auto racing or goat roping, once you start drawing big crowds, big sponsors will soon follow, wallets wide open. In 2001, B.A.S.S. was purchased by TV sports network ESPN...for two reasons. First, because televised fishing tournaments provided hours of cheap programming. Second, because sponsors were willing to pay a load to advertise.

Sponsors were also willing to pay good money to fishermen in the form of cash prizes for tournament winners. It was this seemingly innocent practice that spawned a monster named Danny Engleking.

Engleking lives in Indiana, and that's where he was arrested recently after cheating in a fishing tournament on Indiana's Lake Shafer. Engleking's scheme came to light the day before the tournament began when some amateur anglers spotted some underwater cages in a remote part of the lake...filled with big, fat bass.

Tournament officials were tipped and put up a hidden surveillance camera. On tournament day, they caught the creep red-handed, loading the caged fish into his boat and using them to claim victory.

Cops busted the guy and he went to court for fishing fraud, where he was ordered to pay a $25 fine and $132 in court costs. But he wasn't sentenced to jail...and that's what irks me no end.

No jail? Not good. Catch and release may be good for fish, but where cheating fishers are concerned, it's bad policy.

Modesty Takes a Holiday

Instead of going to the beach, a group of one hundred British college students celebrated the end of the school year by going to an amusement park and then setting a record for putting the most naked people on a roller coaster at one time.

There are so many things wrong with this I don't know where to start.

For my money, naked activities fall into three categories:

1. Things you should do naked. This includes taking a bath.
2. Things you shouldn't do naked. Start with going to church or marching in the 4th of July parade.
3. Things you shouldn't even consider. Riding a roller coaster tops the list.

Others have different notions about nakedness, but I believe my philosophy is sound, since it is based on principles espoused by thee pillars of Western civilization: the Bible, the YMCA and Sir Isaac Newton.

As far as the Bible goes, everyone knows Adam and Eve had a pretty nice lifestyle. Plenty of food, nice place to sleep, no worries about global warming. For them, life was swell right up until Eve convinced Adam to follow some serpent's advice and taste the forbidden fruit. Soon after the first swallow they noticed—for the first time—they were naked, and covered up out of shame. God was so disappointed he kicked them out of the Garden of Eden. If that's not a lesson in the perils of public nudity, nothing is.

As for the YMCA, the new ones are nice and family friendly and fun to visit. The old ones weren't. At least not the YMCA in downtown New Orleans, where my friends and I were sentenced to go swimming every month during elementary school.

At the downtown New Orleans "Y," swimsuits weren't optional. They were totally banned. If you swam at the "Y," you swam in your birthday suit. Period. And always before an audience of elderly gentlemen eager to hand you a towel or offer advice about your backstroke. My friends and I didn't have to be rocket scientists to figure out naked swimming is best left to fish.

And speaking of rocket scientists, the kids who set the naked roller coaster record were all college students. It's fair to assume they were familiar with basic scientific principles, like Sir Isaac Newton's Third Law of Motion, which states that "for every action, there is an equal and opposite reaction."

Nowhere is this more evident than on a rampaging roller coaster. One reason humans wear clothes is to keep body parts from flopping all over the place, which certain parts are prone to do if left at the mercy of gravity. Brassieres and jockey shorts reduce most of these jiggles to a fleshy suggestion, but unfettered body parts on a roller coaster? Look out.

According to Newton's law, when the coaster whips one way, body parts are gonna whip the other way...with gusto. The roller-coasting kids had huge harnesses to keep them in place, but you can bet that with each roll of the coaster, body parts went sailing around like nobody's business. And perhaps causing some unforeseen problems.

"Where did you get that black eye?"

"You wouldn't believe me if I told you."

And besides body parts, there are bodily fluids to be considered, the least of which is perspiration. Once the coaster gets rolling, the adrenaline starts to flow, and once that happens, other things are prone to flow, too. This may be why the amusement park owners insisted the kids sit on fat, fluffy towels during their record-breaking ride.

And if this sounds like a college prank gone mad, it's not. The ride was actually sponsored by the amusement park, which also offered a cash prize for the best group picture of the act.

Call me old-fashioned, but I believe the world was a better place when naked was considered naughty.

Coach

I couldn't tell you what he did for a living or where he lived or if he had a family or not. I just remember that every day at five o'clock, he'd be there. He always wore a clean work shirt and a set of fresh khakis over low-cut work boots. And the hat, of course. A coach has got to have a hat.

Funny thing, though. We never called him Coach. He wouldn't have it. Said he didn't have the qualifications to merit that exalted title, that he was just a man who loved a game and wanted to share that love with a gang of little kids.

We called him Mr. White. He was my first Little League coach. Maybe my best. He didn't know everything there was to know about baseball, but he knew what it took to make it fun for a group of youngsters.

If you needed extra work, he had the time. He'd thump grounders at you until you could swallow those things up in your sleep. He hit fly balls till his arms must have ached, figuring a little repetition never hurt anyone's skills.

He never cursed, he never scolded, he never complained when we blew an easy one-hopper or lost a ball in the sun. We all played in every game, no matter the score or the situation. And though we only won a handful of games the entire spring, it didn't matter one bit. It was baseball, and it was a joy.

Obviously, Little League isn't so joyful anymore. At least around here.

In recent days, Coweta County youth baseball is in the news over incidents that years ago would have been unthinkable and intolerable. We're making statewide headlines because it seems we have some parents who can't go to a ball game without acting more childish than their children.

In one incident, parents came to blows with a coach for pulling their child for a substitute. This, by the way, was in the four- and five-year-old league. In another act of sheer ignorance, some truly macho dude who disagreed with an umpire's call went home, picked up some hardware and came back to the ballpark ready to argue his case at the point of a gun. Fortunately, it didn't come to that, but the mere fact that it could have is cause for alarm.

What rock did these fools crawl out from under? Has our American fascination with sports and sports figures become such a twisted dream that even four-year-olds must be popped into the pressure cooker to make Mom and Dad feel like winners?

It's Little League, folks. It's a game at best. In fact, for most four- and five-year-olds, baseball is still nothing more than a pleasant mystery.

At this level of competition, parents, coaches and umpires alike should be content to watch the wonder in a child's eyes as they capture a slow roller or make an eyes-closed stab on a pop-up. Soon enough these kids will learn the real meaning of competition and the value of the struggle. But before that, they should learn that the games we play as kids are just that. Games. They are not life and death.

Perhaps in light of recent incidents we should take a long look at youth baseball and rethink the whole system. When we have to hire off-duty police to keep order at games, something's out of whack.

This is not what the game was ever intended to be. All it used to take was a ball, a bat and a gang of kids with some time on their hands.

And maybe a level-headed, caring adult or two. Maybe one like Mr. White. But from the looks of things, there aren't many Mr. Whites around these days.

That's too bad for everyone, especially the kids. They don't know what they're missing.

MODERN LIFE

I thought life was tough when I was growing up.
My biggest worries were nuclear bombs, Communists,
civil unrest, and how many girls I'd have to ask for a date
before one choked back her gag reflex and said, "OK. I guess."

Everything seems to be moving faster now. The pressure to be more,
do more, and be perfect in word, deed and selfie
seems relentless. Kids have more access to drugs, premarital sex
is business as usual, and men, women and even children
struggle every day to keep up with their peers and keep
their lives together.

That kind of living comes at a cost. I've met lots of people who paid
way too much for what they got, or wanted to keep.

Hot Time in Health Care

Part of my job is keeping up with strange events. It's fun. It also puts my personal problems in perspective.

Case in point, health care.

Every day, I read stories about medical procedures gone awry, like when a person gets the wrong limb amputated or a newborn baby goes home with somebody else's mama.

For me, the opposite holds true. I realize my body is a temple and should be treated as such, but from time to time I fail to maintain my temple as recommended in the owner's manual.

When something finally breaks, I head for my local health care providers and get it fixed. So far, I've been totally satisfied with the results. No matter the ailment, my health care team—from the stethoscope toters to the nurses to the lab workers to my pharmacists—has kept my carcass in semi-wonderful shape.

I took my excellent care for granted. Not anymore. After reading about the latest health horror, I realize how lucky I am.

When my last ailment popped up, I followed my time-tested procedure and ignored the symptoms until they interfered with watching TV. Then I called the doctor and begged for an appointment.

The diagnosis wasn't disastrous and the prognosis was swell, but as a precaution it was suggested I undergo a procedure designed to detect uninvited visitors in an area of my body that doesn't require sunscreen.

On a cold, gloomy day I hit the hospital at dawn and turned myself over to the local angels of mercy. After a few brief instructions, I was wheeled off to a surgical cubicle were I spent some quality time being roto-rootered. Doctors call this procedure a colonoscopy.

Less than an hour later the fog had cleared and I was ready for a cheeseburger. I went home and didn't give it another thought.

That is, until a recent article from Ananova News Service reminded me of how lucky I was to escape from surgery without turning out like one of the main courses at the Fourth of July barbecue.

Everyone knows medical procedures can have unforeseen side effects, up to and including death. But according to the Ananova story, side effects were somewhat more bizarre for one patient at Virginia Mason Hospital in metro Seattle.

Prior to the surgery, extra alcohol was poured on the patient's chest to kill any loose germs, according to Ananova. But before the alcohol dried completely, the surgeon fired up a power tool that shed a spark that set the alcohol ablaze and turned the patient into a human fireworks display.

The incident was kept quiet until almost two years later when an anonymous letter to the media accused the hospital of tacky care and said the patient had burned to death.

The hospital issued a fierce denial and said the death wasn't caused by the fire at all. It was caused by the heart attack the patient suffered while he was imitating a torch.

Holy lawsuit, Batman.

Reading that story made me extra thankful nothing had gone wrong during my procedure. Especially considering the area being treated. Had someone doused my colon area with alcohol and accidentally set it afire, I could have gone off like a Saturn 5 rocket leaving the launchpad at Cape Canaveral. In fact, I might still be traveling.

I'm glad my health care pals are so professional. But you can't be too careful. Next time I schedule an invasive procedure, I'm going to insist that the surgical team includes a fully equipped firefighter.

Running Scared

The last-minute trip to the beach didn't allow much free time. I spent some of it on a leisurely breakfast at a small curbside cafe. The early October weather matched the fairyland setting, where "cottages" go for a million plus and the people are as pretty as the real estate.

It was early and I had the place to myself except for a trio two tables away, a man, a boy and a girl.

The kids looked to be just shy of school age and fidgeted impatiently as their father, face glowing with a fresh shave, every strand of salt-and-pepper hair groomed to casual perfection, threatened them with arched eyebrows as he tried to chat on his cell phone.

The conversation was strictly business, and it didn't sound like business was good back at the office. As he slammed the phone shut with a soft "Damn!" the kids giggled and said, "Bad word, bad word."

Sensing trouble, I buried my head a little deeper in the morning paper, but before Dad could respond, one of the kids squealed, "Mommy!"

I looked up. Thirty feet down the sidewalk a dark-haired woman was ending her morning run. She waved and gasped, "Just a second," then lifted the designer running tunic to her face, blotting a trickle of perspiration.

She'd pass for gorgeous anywhere. Young, from a distance. Her body was a testament to modern fitness equipment, but small lines around the eyes exposed her as past the sunny side of forty.

She dried herself, sat down and was immediately covered with kids who couldn't wait to tell her about Daddy's bad word. But before she could respond, the lone waitress arrived with food for the father and kids. Dad introduced her by name—Danni, with an "i" —and told his wife how Danni had just earned her business degree and was taking a year off to "live a little bit" before starting that tough climb up the corporate ladder.

Danni flashed a dazzling smile at Dad and turned to take Mom's order. A small tattoo peeked out from the top of the low-slung jeans, and a silver stud winked from a navel carved into a belly as flat and hard as a sheet of steel. The only thing missing was a neon sign screaming, "Young. Sensual. Fertile. Available."

Danni raved about the kids. Mom smiled grimly, nodded, and ordered water and yogurt. Dad wandered off to make another call while Mom tried to manage the kids. The little ones delivered their best one-liners, but Mom only managed a few distracted laughs.

When the waitress wandered back to deliver my plate, Mom shot a quick, nervous glance in Danni's direction. You could almost read her mind.

She's in that gray zone, that vulnerable time when marriages wear thin and a lady's time is split between looking over her shoulder and looking desperately ahead, hoping she makes it to the trust fund finish line with her marriage, and her pride, intact.

From the looks of things her life is good, filled with all the toys and trinkets money can buy. She's the lucky one that grabbed the brass ring. But she knows brass rings tarnish faster these days. She's seen it before with her friends. The wife starts to sag a bit, the younger woman arrives out of no-where and the husband's eyes wander, then his head, then his mailing address.

The meal ended, Dad handed Danni some cash—and his business card—and told her to call when, not if, she decided "to get serious."

The kids were still antsy as Dad buckled them into their car seats. Then he climbed in, started the car and waited for his wife, who stood a few feet away studying the sidewalk.

"You going to ride?" he finally asked.

"No," she said, the forced smile deepening the lines around her eyes. "It's a pretty day. I think I'll run some more."

Snap Judgments

They were good, those dreams. Not the ones where I slew the dragon or scored the winning touchdown, but the others. The sweet, sexy ones. My first effort was probably in the fifth grade, when I wondered for weeks what it would be like to rub lips with June Johnson.

It turned out the dreaming was better than the doing, so I kept doing what I did best. I eventually reached the point where I could fantasize a grand romance at the drop of a hint.

But time teaches some hard lessons, and as the hair thinned and the belly thickened, the fantasies became tiresome. So I found a new game to play.

These days I watch and I listen and I wonder, inventing make-believe lives for total strangers who catch my attention. A few weeks ago, I was at it again.

I was in a new town and it was late and I was bored, so I decided to take a stroll through London's trendy Notting Hill district. After an hour or so I had walked up an appetite, but the pubs had closed for the night, so I popped into a small café attached to a large hotel.

She worked behind the bar, and the small brass badge on her pocket identified her as Natalie. She was tall, thirtyish, not gorgeous but certainly attractive, with no visible scars, marks, tattoos or piercings and no ring to identify her as either promised or married. Behind her dark eyes was a hint of attitude, a touch of mystery that got my attention. I started watching and playing "I wonder."

She was polite but not chatty, unusual in one of the few places in town where tips were actively solicited. When she wasn't mixing a drink or pushing a pint of ale across the bar to Eva, the table waitress, she looked at her watch and ran her fingers nervously through her thick, black hair.

Obviously something was on her mind. What, I wondered. The job? Kids? Money? A man?

By now I was hooked, and the questions began to tumble through my mind. Who loves Natalie, I wondered? Who loves her and holds her close? Whose soft touch and gentle whispers help her forget, at least for a moment, the grim reality of life's everyday nightmares?

Who loves Natalie, with the bright white shirt and short black skirt and sensible shoes with the thin ankle straps and small brass buckles?

I wondered where she lived. Was it a snug little cottage with a warm fire to keep London's perpetual chill at bay or a cold-water flat with sheets for curtains and thin cotton blankets? Did she sleep alone and like it or share a bed and wish she didn't?

As she worked, her expression rarely changed. She kept her bar customers tended to and filled Eva's table orders calmly and quickly.

By the time I finished my snack, I had it figured. She was freshly divorced, dumped by some guy who had used her hard then left for somebody with fewer wrinkles or more money. There were kids, too, and a new man, and she was anxious to get home and make sure the children were safe and the man was still interested.

When a soft chime announced last call, I kept watching and wondering if I had gotten it right.

I didn't have to wonder long. As the last customer cleared his tab, Natalie and Eva split what little change there was in the tip jar. Natalie slipped on her sweater and grabbed her bag, then leaned over and gave Eva a big kiss. On the mouth. They walked out hand in hand, Eva's head on Natalie's shoulder.

Sometimes I get it right. Sometimes I get it wrong. This time, I got the feeling I needed to find another game to play.

Time for Some Girl Talk

The biggest problem with getting old is losing stuff—like your teeth and your hair and your mind. But there is also a silver lining to being silver-haired. As you age, it's easier to fool folks, especially young people.

The older I get, the more I find young people seeking my advice, mostly so they can do exactly the opposite. This is especially true in the field of romance. It happened again the other day when a young female acquaintance asked for suggestions about a personal problem.

OK, she didn't exactly ask me personally, but I was close enough to eavesdrop while she was asking a fellow female for romantic tips. Being a loving, caring kind of guy, I immediately volunteered to help.

My offer sent her rushing to the restroom, but after a brief bout of nausea, she returned and said she would be willing to at least listen to my advice before ignoring it.

My young friend has a problem common to many twentysomething chicks. She knows several young men she finds attractive, but so far the dudes have been either (a) too self-absorbed, (b) too preoccupied or (c) too stupid to ask her out. She wanted to know if there was a tasteful and discreet way she can drop the hint that she's interested.

The answer is yes. And the procedure is relatively easy. The problem is making sure you're dangling your bait in front of the right fish. While I'm sure my lady friend would not be influenced by such frivolous things as good looks and a quick wit, some immature females are often impressed by these superficial qualities.

Forget it, girls. More experienced women will tell you that a man's real attractiveness increases in direct proportion to the size of his bank account.

But enough about picking a man. Once you're sure he's the one for you, the next step is making sure he's aware of that fact.

Let's start at the beginning. Remember, girls, first impressions count. If you want to snag a man, start out by trying not to look like one. Combat boots were fine for Seattle area rockers with unshaven armpits, but when a woman is on the prowl, she should look her feminine best.

You don't want to look trashy, but I think any decent man would be attracted to a woman wearing nice four-inch spike heels below a miniskirt and fishnet stockings.

Showing a little cleavage doesn't hurt, either. A little. My motto is, "Once he's looked, he's hooked." Getting noticed is half the battle.

The other half is acting like you don't know you've been noticed. This is vital, girls. Play it cool, play it coy, play it shy. Acting disinterested will drive a guy wild. If it doesn't, chances are he's not good date material, anyway.

Once you get his attention, the question is, how to keep it? This is where most chicks flop because they haven't mastered the art of talking to men. It's really not that tricky. To make a man think you're sexy, fascinating, wonderful and everything else he's ever dreamed of, just get him to talk about himself.

Guys can do this for hours. They will tell you their bowling scores, their golf handicaps and, if they really like you, their favorite fishing lure. When they've gone that far, the game is over and you can reel 'em in.

And that's all there is to it. Another caution, however. Many young ladies tell me that even guys who look good on paper think they look better between the sheets and aren't hesitant to inquire about a girl's inclinations in this area.

Let me say this. If you're serious about a guy, just say no! If he's serious about you, he won't mind. A real gentleman would never ask to test drive a Rolls-Royce.

Sexy Swedes Setting Wrong Kind of Record

They called it "The Summer of Love." Probably because, in 1967, America wasn't quite ready to embrace an event called "Fornication Fest."

And that's exactly what it was. In 1967, "Sex, drugs and rock & roll" wasn't an aging cliché but the urgent aspiration of the founders of America's hippie movement, who set out dressed in tie-dyed duds and warped by brain-bruising chemicals to prove that "All You Need Is Love."

And they weren't talking about the love-for-your-fellow-man variety. The Summer of Love was all about the kind of hot, steamy sex that, until then, had been tucked firmly away in America's cultural closet.

The home office for this global love-in was San Francisco, but not because the dope and rent were dirt cheap in the city's Haight-Ashbury district. It was held in San Francisco because you couldn't drive a Volkswagen van to Sweden.

Openly promiscuous premarital sex was a novel idea to most Americans, but by the mid-sixties, the word Sweden was synonymous with casual sex. And according to what I heard, it was all true. I spent part of the summer of '65 traveling with a group of exchange students from all over the world. There wasn't a Swede in the group, but we did have a Finn. And the American kids in the group never tired of hearing Hannu Miettenen ramble on about the "easy" ways of his next-door Swedish neighbors.

I couldn't believe it was true. Apparently, it was. Looks like the Swedes have been making out like minks on death row. But now they're learning that "free love" carries a pretty hefty price tag. A price Swedes are paying daily as they contract certain sexually transmitted diseases (STDs) at record rates.

A Swedish favorite is chlamydia. This disease can be cured, but because the symptoms often go unnoticed for too long, chlamydia often causes major problems, like infertility in women. In the year 2003, 26,800 Swedes—almost three percent of the population—contracted this disease.

By way of context, figures from the Centers for Disease Control show that in 2002, Americans were infected with chlamydia at one-tenth the rate of Swedes. This kind of statistic doesn't make anyone proud, especially the Swedes. So they've set out to solve the STD problem—by creating a service that gives a whole new meaning to the term "when the rubber meets the road."

They call it the Cho-San Express. If the name sounds like an Asian fast-food delivery service, that's not far from the truth. The Cho-San Express delivers all right. But not anything you'd want to eat.

The express is a fleet of government owned and operated vans, four in Stockholm and two each in Gothenburg and Malmo, Sweden's next two largest cities.

Painted with a large red rubber (complete with wings), the vans are crammed with condoms, and between the hours of 4 p.m. and 9 p.m., Swedish lovers who are feeling frisky but lack protection can whip out their cell phones and call the Cho-San condom-mobile. In minutes a handy ten pack of farm-fresh condoms will arrive at their door.

This idea was hatched by a Swedish ministry called the Organization for Sexual Education. Spokesperson Carl Osvald insisted the new condom-delivery campaign is more than a way to protect against the spread of disease. "With this campaign, we believe that we will reach young people with a humorous twinkle in their eye," he said. "It's our hope that the contraceptive will be perceived as a fun sex accessory."

A "fun sex accessory." Oh, for the good old days, when the only thing that qualified as a sex accessory had a heartbeat.

Time changes things. Even travel plans. Years ago, I longed to visit Sweden. I might still go, but if I do, I'll stick to the sightseeing. The worst I could catch is a cold.

The First Commandment of Romance

At best, we were Budweiser buddies. A couple of guys who'd struck up a few conversations that turned into a few more until maybe we thought we knew each other. Too many evenings bruising elbows together on polished pine bar tops can do that to you.

And so this particular night, after we'd finished dissecting the Falcons and the Braves and exhausting our usual repertoire of small talk, he just up and started in on his love life.

Frankly, I'd thought the guy was single. No ring or tattoo or identifying marks to announce otherwise. Turns out, though, he was married, and had been for a while.

But he wasn't happy, he said, and she wasn't happy, and recently, he and she had gone from separate bedrooms to separate mailboxes, and like he said, he wasn't happy about it.

He didn't furnish any details of the split, just showed me his side of the relationship's coin. He's a young guy and obviously does well, as he's always swimming in stuff. He said he'd shared it with her, kept her well roofed and covered with all the niceties, including the fine jewelry, the expensive clothes, and the four-thousand-pound full-length black wrap with a Mercedes label.

So they had their stuff and they thought it was enough. Trouble was, they'd spent no time on the inside, sharing secrets, stroking egos, doing the hard work. He said he knew it needed to get done but figured it would just happen, that one day their souls would take wing and Happily-Ever-After would arrive, Special Delivery.

So far that load of happy hasn't been delivered. Still, they're working at it. They go for counseling. They meet and they talk and they try, he said, but so far, no positive results.

So over a called third strike during the Braves game, he asks me, "How can this happen?" I told him to seek advice elsewhere, that my romantic record reads more rap sheet than rhapsody, but he just laughed and said hey, you've been around, you must have picked up something. I gave him what I had.

I told him I'd learned there's nothing fairy tale about a relationship. That good men and good women can, despite the best intentions, come to bad ends.

I told him the stuff I'd picked up from late-night TV and the occasional volume of self-help. And then I told him the real stuff, that when the flames leap and the lightning strikes, all the rules go out the window because you think with your heart and not your head. And then one day, BAM! The lightning stops and the thunder fades and the monsoon ends.

And when the dry season sets in and you find yourself face-to-face with someone and the time comes to actually build a life together, both parties better be equipped with full emotional toolboxes.

I thought it was pretty good stuff in a "Those who can't do, teach" sort of way. He seemed impressed. We ordered another beer and watched the Braves lose. In a parting gesture, I told him if he really wanted things to work out, he'd have to keep digging, to work for it, work hard. He thought a minute and said he had one job and wasn't sure he wanted to tackle another.

So he headed back to his place alone to maybe ponder the workings of love, or at least what suit to wear on his rounds tomorrow.

I didn't tell him the whole story. After all, a young guy needs to figure some things out for himself. One of these days, after a few more tumbles and tosses, he'll learn that one final lesson. The one that only experience teaches.

There ain't no gentle cycle on the washing machine of love.

Why, Indeed?

The planning is brutal, the service is short and, statistically speaking, the result is tentative. So why, after all this time, do couples still insist on committing matrimony?

Could be the valentine displays in the stores or the fact that a couple of my coworkers are planning for one, but for some reason I've been wondering about weddings. Mostly about how this strange ritual came to be, and why?

Actually, the why is a no-brainer. Let's face it, men are pigs, and for most of human history, a wedding vow was the only solvent strong enough to remove a stubborn set of bloomers.

Of course, it wasn't always that way. Adam and Eve came from the factory naked and thought nothing of it until that first bite of apple sent them in search of leafy loincloths. It seems that soon after, the concept of marriage was launched.

My colleague Angela did some rapid research on the elder Testament and ascertained that by the time Noah set sail, the in-law habit had developed. And so it remained for millennia. When it came to romance, a guy had to say "I do" before he heard "I will."

In the sixties, that changed as a large chunk of the Woodstock generation introduced us to cheap drugs, bad hair and the concept of Free Love (which in most cases was not, if you included the cost of penicillin). Unfortunately, I was not among the naked dope-smokers and spent most of an entire school year plowing through the petticoats of the fabulous Darlene Dawson, searching for the holy grail of lust. It wasn't pretty.

"Come on, baby. I looove you. Promise."

"I said forget it, you oversexed pig."

"But baby, I loooooooooooove you. And I've always thought you looked great in beige. Pink, too."

"Can the compliments, you jerk. I plan on wearing white at my wedding. When the ring hits the finger, the clothes hit the floor and not a second sooner."

Of course that dialogue sounds dated today. In fact, these days, sadly, a large segment of society barely yawns at premarital sex, much less premarital children. Still, couples persist in tying the knot. And getting married is no easy task.

You give a woman a wedding date and there is never enough time. For a budding bride, there is much to do. There are bridesmaids to be chosen, and wedding gowns, music to be selected and flowers to be picked, decisions to be made about caterers, photographers, china patterns and whether or not to assault guests with birdseed or rice.

The groom's role, though different, is equally exhausting. He is charged with making sure that the wedding date does not conflict with a really important event such as an SEC football game or the Daytona 500. He also plans the honeymoon, seeing to such romantic matters as the temperature of the beer in the motel lounge, whether or not the room rate includes free movie channels and if the mattress comes equipped with a coin-operated magic fingers machine.

Finally the Big Day arrives. And after weeks, months, sometimes years of preparation, the comatose couple drifts through a fifteen-minute ceremony, slices an overpriced cake and heads out for that dream honeymoon.

By this time the poor bride is too exhausted to think, much less enjoy the complimentary wine in the motel lounge or her choice of in-room movies. And as she hits the sack, the befuddled groom is left with a beer in one hand and the remote in the other, hoping that ESPN will be showing a rerun of last year's Daytona 500.

Yep, it's tough, but people do it. And I guess deep down, I really know why. Marriage is hard work, but on the other hand...

All in favor of a lifetime of blind dates, raise your hand.

The Language of Love

A long, long time ago everybody in the world spoke the same language. It had lots of words like "Thee" and "Thou" and "Shalt."

Then along came a silly little king who got too big for his britches. He decided to build a tower all the way to Heaven so he could talk to God face-to-face. What a jerk.

Load after load of stuff came in from the Desert Depot building supply, and thousands of workers toiled for years building a monument to stupidity.

God watched and, after He'd had a good laugh, decided to put an end to the foolishness. He did it in a rather amusing way. He just caused all the workers to start speaking in different languages.

This created some major construction problems. Such oft-used phrases as "Oh, Raoul, here's that red-hot rivet you asked for," were translated into a co-worker's new language as "Hey, you dimwitted camel jockey, stick this where the sun don't shine."

The Tower of Babel was never finished. The world lost an architectural landmark but gained something much better: a whole new set of languages like English, French, German, Japanese and Rap.

My favorite is English, which is what I speak. It works fine except when you go overseas where a lot of people speak foreign. But that's not usually a big problem because you can get pocket dictionaries to translate just about anything. You can get English to Chinese, English to Hindu, even English to Polish, which is considered a language even though it doesn't have any vowels.

Lately, it's occurred to me we need one more of these dictionaries: English to Female. Female is tricky. It sounds like English, but it doesn't make any sense, because in Female, words have different meanings.

In regular English, if your buddies say, "We need to talk," you figure it's time to decide something important like who's bringing the ribs to the game or where you'll be fishing over the weekend.

But a woman says, "We need to talk," and you've got trouble. It usually means you've done a big no-no like leave the toilet seat up or forgotten an anniversary or, God forbid, failed to notice the new hairdo.

And when a woman says, "I want to get something off my chest," she's not talking about having a tattoo removed. In most cases, anyway.

Lots of times, women will speak Female to try and stump you with trick questions. One of their favorites is, "Tell me how you feel."

Here's a hint, boys. Do not say, "A little bloated, but mostly fine."

The correct response is something like, "My heart overflows with wonder that every day I am allowed to walk in the shadow of your wondrous presence, content to drown like a possum carcass in the whirlpool of your love."

But the most treacherous use of Female is when women say something and no matter what you say back, it's gonna be wrong.

Like, if she says, "You're not sensitive to my needs," and you say, "Hey, I just rotated your tires," be prepared to hear, "See, that's what I mean. Why can't you be like Phil Donahue or Alan Alda? You're a stupid, insensitive man who doesn't understand anything. I'm talking about my needs, not my vehicle. I need you to send me flowers and tell me I'm still pretty and desirable and not fat and you can't live without me."

"Well, OK, sweetie. You look just as pretty to me as the day we met."

"WAAAHHH!!!"

"What's the matter now?"

"Everybody knows we met at the zit clinic the day after I was crowned Swine Princess at the county fair."

"Oh."

Sometimes I think it's hopeless. If Funk & Wagnalls doesn't put in some serious overtime on that dictionary, I don't know what we guys will do. I know one thing, though. If you're a male and you don't make every effort to learn how to speak Female, sooner or later you're guaranteed to hear one certain word that needs no translation...

"Goodbye."

ME AND THE LORD.
A WORK IN PROGRESS.

I told one of my preachers once that I felt like I'd spent my life proving I couldn't do anything right until I'd done everything wrong. It wasn't a random thought.

I'm finally getting better. I make an effort to get closer to God every day. So far, He's been very patient. I hope that doesn't change.

You Want Fries With That Sermon?

The four years I spent in Alexandria, Louisiana, were among the best of my life. It was there I played my first notes of music and my first innings of Little League ball. It was there I learned to shoot squirrels and catch crawfish and ride a horse bareback.

And it was there I started blazing through puberty like a heat-seeking missile. The sight of me in a perpetual state of hormonal overdrive convinced Mother to drag me to church every time the doors creaked open.

Emmanuel Baptist became like a second home, and although I wasn't the most pious adolescent, I never minded going. The services didn't interest me, but the breaks between scheduled events were fabulous.

Across the street from the church was a place called Shipley Do-Nuts. The front of the shop featured a massive plate glass window that allowed viewers to witness the creation of some of the best donuts on earth.

Between Sunday School and church my friends and I would stand there and drool as endless ranks of uncooked donuts dropped from a gleaming steel rack into a huge tub of sizzling grease where they bubbled and boiled before bobbing in golden brown goodness to the surface.

The sizzling hot treats were then baptized in a river of melted, gooey sugar. They were absolutely delicious, especially when hot. The donut makers made sure that on Sunday morning, the hot ones kept coming. We stuffed ourselves.

At the time, eating donuts was not considered a major health risk—much less a sin—so Mother let me have as many as my allowance could stand. With one exception.

Once a month the church observed the Lord's Supper, the Baptist version of Holy Communion. Toward the end of the ceremony, deacons delivered tiny chips of unleavened bread and thimble-sized glasses of Welch's Concord Grape Juice.

On those Sundays, mother banned donuts, fearing they would ruin my appetite for the righteous, if somewhat skimpy, feast. When it came to church and food, Mother was a stickler for tradition.

I wonder what she would think of recent goings-on at a Houston church. I imagine she'd be horrified at the thought of the Lord's Supper being catered by Ronald McDonald.

Jesus said it was our duty to feed the hungry, and Houston's Brentwood Baptist Church took Him at His word. And at feeding time, this church doesn't have to look far for empty stomachs. Brentwood Baptist's 7,000 members are busy day and night seven days a week with worship services, mission studies, youth activities, senior citizens meetings and just about anything else you can think of.

As attendance soared, feeding the multitudes became a concern. Local businessman and church member Ernest Redmond finally solved the problem. Redmond owned six McDonald's in the Houston area and figured a seventh wouldn't hurt so he decided to install a Mickey D's in the church's new community center. The restaurant is co-owned by the church and comes complete with a drive-in window for the Christian on the go.

I'm familiar with the concept of separation of church and state, but I wonder how our founding fathers would have felt about separation of church and Big Mac. We may soon find out. After all, the local community will be patronizing the holy McDonald's, too.

There could be trouble the first time a heathen drives up and hears, "You want some salvation with those fries?"

Giving It Up for Lent

This year I made it two whole weeks without having to admit the awful truth to anyone. But the other day, I was in the break room at work when a co-worker came up and asked, "What did you give up for Lent?"

I hung my head in shame and mumbled, "Nothing."

"Nothing?" she said. "I don't know how you can live with yourself. Everybody gives up something for Lent."

"But I'm not Catholic," I stammered...

"Wake up, bonehead. The Dark Ages are over. Everybody does Lent these days."

I said I was sorry and asked what she had given up.

"Cigarettes!" she hissed. "But I wish I'd given up talking to you. In fact, I just have."

She left, and I pondered the matter. I knew I could have tried to give something up, and I know it's probably a good practice to give up a good thing from time to time, but every time I tried I just couldn't do it right. I gave up Krispy Kremes once but left a loophole for Dunkin' Donuts, so I figure it didn't really count. Other attempts were equally fruitless. I could say I'm just weak, but the truth is, Lent has not been good to me.

Until I was 10 I lived in New Orleans, which has since been officially taken over by the mafia and space aliens but at the time was heavily Catholic.

The demographic makeup of the Crescent City caused great concern for my mother, a devout Southern Baptist and South Georgia girl who had probably never seen a Catholic before she was grown, and regarded them with great suspicion.

During our stay in New Orleans, Mother kept a close eye on my comings and goings and warned me about getting too close to any followers of the Pope.

"But Mom," I whined, "most of the kids around here are Catholics, and I play with them and they're all nice to me."

"They're just trying to convert you," she said. "Watch out."

I checked myself almost daily for any signs of backsliding, but I kept associating with Catholics, especially my friend Lenny Delcazel. Lenny was so Catholic he actually went to a Catholic school. But he still seemed nice. Until one day...

We were playing marbles in front of the apartment and Lenny asked, "What did you give up for Lent?"

"What's Lent?" I asked.

"You don't know about Lent? You didn't give nothin' up? You're gonna go to the devil," he said matter-of-factly. "What religion are you, anyway?"

"Baptist," I said, rather hesitantly.

"Yep. That does it. You're a goner for sure."

I was beginning to get nervous and asked if he was sure. "Yep," he said. "Straight to Hell."

"Stay here," I screamed and ran into the house. I emerged moments later, holding my most precious possession. I showed it to Lenny and said, "If I give this up, will I be OK?"

He looked it over. "Yeah, this ought to do it," he said.

"Who do I give it to?" I asked.

"I'll take care of it," he said and walked off with my brand-new Superman comic book.

That one hurt, but a later Lent was even more painful.

It was my senior year in high school, and I'd been dating Darlene Dawson a few weeks, but so far my romantic efforts had been rewarded with nothing more than a few steamy, and altogether too brief, kisses.

As we sat at the drive-in theater one night, I eased my arm around her and said, "Hey, Darlene, it's almost Lent. You thought about it?"

"Yeah," she said, "I just can't think of a single thing. What do you think I ought to give up?"

When I told her what I had in mind, she gave me a shot to the ribs that left me wheezing for weeks.

Since then I have mostly avoided Lent altogether. A little confession may be good for the soul, but a little pain, I can live without. And as far as I'm concerned, Lent hurts.

Prayers Can Be Precarious

At first, the new apartment not far from Lake Pontchartrain was an adventure. Then I got scarlet fever. The adventure turned into a prison sentence. I prayed to be set free.

After I was diagnosed, the New Orleans Health Department posted a bright yellow "Quarantine!" sign on the front door. No one was allowed in. And we weren't allowed out. Officially. I think the school truant officer came by once and caught my sister playing in the yard.

When Marilyn told him her brother had a highly contagious, sometimes lethal disease, he left.

I kept praying to be set free. By the time I was declared non-toxic again, I had learned something about watching what I prayed for. Since then—except for that first date with Sandra Bowman in the 11th grade—I've tried to keep my prayers as unselfish as possible.

These days, I pray for other people to do well or get better when they're sick. I pray for our soldiers at home and abroad. I pray for good weather for farmers.

I don't pray to win the lottery. And not just because it would be selfish. If I expect God to listen to me, I certainly ought to listen to Him, and that's something I don't do nearly well enough.

But sometimes, I'm still tempted.

I rise before sunup these days and always spend a minute or two on the porch where it's cool and quiet. The other day, though, I couldn't enjoy the predawn peace. I was too terrified.

It's not unusual for me to come up with a bad idea for a column. But this day, I didn't have an idea at all.

It was a big concern. Before I knew it, I found myself hovering on the brink of a totally selfish prayer request. But before the words formed, I was distracted by a strange sound in the bushes under the window.

The critters are abundant near my place, and noises in the shrubs are commonplace. But this was different. It wasn't the quick, raspy scratching of a squirrel on the move or the papery fluttering of a bird about to take wing. This was a slower, rumbling rattle of brush.

I heard the noise again and looked down. A dim shape began to creep from beneath the begonias. At first I thought it was the neighbor's cat, which prowls the shrubbery from time to time. But as the shape emerged

into the moonlight, it was bigger, longer and much fatter than the neighbor's cat.

Then the clouds cleared, the full moon blazed and there it was: a possum. One of the biggest, ugliest specimens of this species I've ever seen.

And it was headed straight for me. The creature crept out of the grass and onto the sidewalk, then swiveled around smooth as you please and stared me right in the face.

I didn't know what to do, so I looked down and said, "Hello."

Its beady eyes narrowed, and it took another step forward.

"Boo," I barked, hoping the beast would back off. Instead, the possum hissed scornfully and advanced again, its beady eyes glowing in the pale light.

It reached the bottom of the steps. I was reaching inside the front door for the broom to defend myself when, to my great relief, the possum looked up, shook its head, snorted and sauntered down the sidewalk and across the street toward the dumpster.

It left me shaken but relieved that I hadn't wasted a perfectly good prayer on a column idea. At least I hoped I hadn't. I wasn't quite sure whether I'd sent that wish off or not. And I sure couldn't blame Him, but I'd hate to think God answered my prayer with a possum.

Actions Speak Louder

She never set out to make the headlines. But on December 30, 2002, Martha Myers was front-page news all over the world. For all the wrong reasons. I read the story a little more closely than most. You tend to do that when you know the subject.

We were more church buddies than pals when we were in high school together. Martha was a few years older and closer to my sister. The families were friends, and Martha's father, a former Alabama state health official, wrote a letter of recommendation that helped my sister get into medical school, where she and Martha were classmates.

Martha went directly into the Southern Baptist foreign mission service after medical school. It was over a dozen years later that my sister, along with her husband and three children, followed the same path. When I visited my sister in Korea, she said she saw Martha several times a year at mission conferences in Sri Lanka or Bangkok or some other far-flung outpost. She often mentioned Martha in her letters home and genuinely admired her friend's faith and devotion to her calling.

Martha Myers had been in Yemen for 25 years and, according to those who knew her best, loved the country and its people. She worked at a Baptist hospital that served over 40,000 patients a year.

She knew it wasn't safe work. After her death, family members recalled that about four years ago, Martha had been carjacked while driving one of the hospital's vehicles. Martha refused to get out, so the bandits threw her in the back of the van, covered her with a blanket and drove off. Later, when the vehicle hit an obstruction and was disabled, the thieves ran off and left Martha with the van.

She had told stories about grenades thrown onto the hospital grounds and said that it wasn't unusual to have threats issued against the hospital or its workers, on strictly religious grounds.

She was in the United States on furlough September 11, 2001 and saw that Muslim anger against Americans was rising in Yemen and around the world. Three months later, she returned to Yemen anyway, saying it was where God wanted her to be.

She loved it so much that years ago, she expressed a desire to be buried there. That's one wish that came true. It's comforting to know that when Martha Myers' body was taken from the hospital, hundreds of patients and local people lined the streets out of respect. And it's comforting to know that she was there by choice doing the thing she loved best.

And it's comforting to know that from printed statements, her family members had enough class, or compassion, not to condemn Ali Abdulrazzak al-Kamel, the man who has been arrested and charged with Martha Myers' death. Wish I were that big a person. I'm not.

After his arrest, the killer said he acted out of a desire to "cleanse his church and to get closer to god" (small "g" intentional). To me, that sounds like pure hatred. Or pure insanity.

A man whose opinion and knowledge of the Muslim religion I respect calls me to task frequently for making what he considers insensitive and misguided remarks about Islam. He says it is truly a religion of peace, hope and kindness. Maybe he's right. But if so, then this is one religion that is having a hell of a problem getting the message out.

Hope, peace and kindness? When Martha Myers' religion called on her to show her love, she did it by serving others until she was killed for her trouble. If there are Muslims doing the same thing, someone please let me know.

I'm sure Martha Myers has long since forgiven her killer and the religion he says drove him to commit murder. Maybe I'd like to do the same someday. But right now, I wouldn't count on it.

Nothing Holy in the News Biz These Days

If it happened today, would it read like this?

JACKSON, Miss.—Authorities on Thursday began court-ordered sanity hearings for a young mother known to the press only as Mary.

According to court records, preliminary psychiatric studies found her to be sane, even though she has pleaded guilty to charges of child cruelty after authorities discovered that she recently gave birth to a young child in an unheated barn on the outskirts of her husband's hometown of Tupelo.

This case has held the nation's attention ever since the woman appeared on *Larry King Live* and insisted that the child, a boy, was not the result of a romantic encounter with her husband. Mary claims she was impregnated by a supernatural being and says she was unaware of the fertilization until notified of the act by an "angel" who identified himself as Gabriel.

Her husband, Joseph, an itinerant woodworker, backs up his wife's account and has confirmed that prior to the pregnancy, the couple had never consummated their marriage. He simply says, "Mary's a good person, and if that's what she says happened, I believe her."

Women's rights groups around the country have rushed to Mary's defense, saying the young woman is a victim of the system. Ms. Freda Flamethrower, president of the Coalition For Babes, stated, "So the chick's off her rocker. That doesn't make her any less qualified to be a mother. It's all a plot by a bunch of old men to keep a sister down."

Men's groups have been no less vocal. Sid Studly, Chairman of Guys, Inc., says, "We believe that the child comes first. Obviously the baby cannot be raised by a lunatic who claims her child is the son of ET."

Scientists at the Massachusetts Institute of Technology, commenting on the woman's claim of virgin birth, said that despite reoccurring myths by fringe groups, scientific studies have proven that virgin conception is impossible. They said that births to lesbian women, who are technically virgins in the male/female sense, don't count, as they were only accomplished with the aid of a male sperm donor.

One of the most puzzling aspects of the case is the young woman's insistence that the child is actually of unearthly origin, or as she puts it, "the Son of God."

Scholars are not surprised at the claim. A Midwestern expert on the occult stated, "Throughout history there have been legends of messiahs, or saviors, sent to earth by unknown deities to perform certain works down here. These reports generally coincide with some global event, such as the upcoming millennium." He went on to say that he wouldn't be surprised to hear more of these claims as the year 2001 approaches.

And in a bizarre related tale, three retired auto parts executives were being held for questioning after they were detained just north of Tupelo, driving a Ryder rental truck packed with gifts.

Police first suspected the goods were stolen, but credit card receipts showed the materials had been legally purchased. Police became suspicious when the three men reported they were on their way to deliver the gifts but admitted they did not know who the gifts were intended for or where they would find the recipient.

One of the men stated, "We just had a feeling." They apparently were following the new star that has appeared recently in Southern skies.

Regarding the star, meteorologists are still puzzled by its appearance but say it is probably related to the recent weather disturbances in the Pacific region.

The infant remains in court custody while the case is under investigation.

Signs and Wonders

I believe that one of these days God will say, "Game Over," chalk up His cue stick and stroke this miserable planet right into a corner pocket of the universe. I believe it will surely happen. I just don't believe humans can predict when. Not that some haven't tried.

One of the gloom and doom hall-of-famers is Nostradamus, who died several hundred years ago after predicting many things, including the end of our world. I'm sure he meant well, but as far as I know, he had as many misses as hits, and buying burial acreage based on his predictions makes as much sense as taking stock tips from a flying squirrel.

Countless others have claimed to see the end in visions filled with fires, floods and earthquakes. And it seems that every time the calendar takes a giant leap, the predictions of global annihilation get worse. Turns of the century are bad. The end of a millennium is worse.

Visions change with the times. These days, most prophets claim we'll be done in by a few faulty computer chips.

Sorry, but I can't buy it. I guess I'm just not one for signs and wonders. Or I wasn't until recently.

It was a pretty weekend day, the weather was mild, the breeze was high, and outside the window a pear tree was birthing some premature blooms. Things were pretty normal for my little piece of the universe. Then I saw something that gave me a start, as strange a sight as I've ever seen.

The big robin was on patrol, hopping around in the sunshine with the wind ruffling his downy red breast, mining the lawn for a fat worm. He snagged one, a specimen large enough for me to see clearly from a window twenty feet away. I watched, thinking it would be interesting to see how he'd handle the oversized entree.

But before he could eat, up came the cat. It was new to me, a kitten really, maybe three or four months old. It didn't have a collar, wasn't any recognizable breed and appeared to be pretty much on its own. You can tell sometimes.

Here comes trouble, I thought. I waited, expecting the cat to pounce and the bird to fly away or get nailed.

It never happened. The bird saw the cat, hopped back a step, looked it square in the face and just stood there. The kitten walked slowly towards the bird, got within four feet or so and instead of springing, simply sat down. The bird cocked its head, swallowed the worm and did something amazing. It walked over to the kitten. The kitten's tail started to twitch and I thought again, uh-oh, this is it.

I was about to tap on the window to scare the bird off but stopped when I saw what was happening. The two creatures were nose-to-nose, but the cat didn't hiss, the robin didn't chirp. They just looked at each other. The cat gave a small shake and the bird took a hop, but for most of a minute they just sat there and looked at each other.

Finally, the bird flew off and the cat lay down in a sunny spot and dozed.

It wasn't exactly the lion lying down with the lamb, but it wasn't exactly normal behavior for predator and prey, either.

Maybe it meant something and maybe it didn't. And maybe this strange behavior doesn't mean the end is near. But to me it was a sign that things aren't what they used to be.

Which doesn't mean I believe all the current doomsday predictions, but still, I may start paying closer attention to my churchgoing habits.

No matter what happens, it sure couldn't hurt.

WORDS AND MUSIC

I've always been fond of words. I was reading as soon as I could hold up the Sunday comics and still don't let a day pass without a healthy dose of words, old and new.

The only thing I ever loved as much as words is music. Mother told me I started jamming to what she called "the classics" when I was still penned up in the crib, so I guess it came naturally. But when I started playing a musical instrument, my life changed forever.

The man who changed it was Johnny Long. Today he's Dr. Johnny Long. He's retired but still holds the title of Director of Bands Emeritus at Troy University's John M. Long School of Music.

He was my band director at Robert E. Lee High School in Montgomery, Alabama, and later at what was then Troy State University.

He will always be the most influential man in my life. Johnny Long's gift wasn't so much teaching music as making you believe you could do anything—including playing any piece of music he put in front of you. He believed in his students and made us believe in ourselves. I've never been prouder or had more fun than when I was in one of Johnny Long's bands.

Over the years Dr. Long has made music a pleasure for generations of students. I've never heard one say a bad word about him. Johnny Long didn't just help me make music, he made music a part of my life. It still is. A day doesn't go by that I don't think about Johnny Long and his impact on my life.

This chapter is titled "Words and Music." The stories in this section were inspired by the music from some of my favorite golden oldies.

"Bend Me, Shape Me"
American Breed, 1968

I should have known better than to trust a strange woman with my body.

She said it would be gentle and pleasant, and at first, it was. But after five minutes, a trickle of sweat appeared on my brow. In ten minutes it was a torrent. She ignored it, urging me on until my breath came in gasps and a roar filled my ears. It was unlike anything I'd ever felt before.

That one encounter made it very clear. Yoga was hell.

I guess I took it up out of boredom as much as anything. I was between jobs and marriages, with no money to spend but plenty of time to spare. I spent hours watching TV, and the yoga lady washed up on my set during some predawn channel surfing.

She wore black tights and had a pleasant face and a soothing voice that convinced me yoga might be enjoyable. Her gentle stretching movements were graceful and looked like they'd be easy on an aging set of bones. She said repeatedly that breathing was important, and I already knew how to do that, so I figured I was halfway home.

I was in decent shape then, walked a few miles each weekday, more on weekends. I rode the bike some. The legs were good, the lungs were OK and while I wasn't exactly Mr. America, I wasn't walrus boy, either.

I knew if the TV chick could handle it, so could I.

I watched her and followed along. We began by settling into the lotus position. At first glance, the lotus seems innocent enough. You simply sit down, cross one leg, and then cross the other leg over the one you crossed to begin with.

If you do it right, you wind up with your right foot on your left knee, your left foot on your right knee and, in my case, a grimace on your face.

Guys obviously aren't intended to bend that way. At least I wasn't. I grabbed the first foot and dragged it to a knee, and the leg dutifully followed. Then I grabbed the other foot and trouble began. The second leg had to go higher up and around the first leg and it just wasn't working. I grunted and strained and things looked bleak for a moment, but I had the heart of a champion and didn't quit until my feet rested on my knees.

About then I understood why breathing was so important. You need lots of air to support all the screams of pain. Halfway through the thirty-minute session, I was squealing like a pig and puffing like a Lamaze student. And I was twisted into a shape God never intended for man.

I can't quite describe it, but I think the position I had assumed is still illegal in 27 states and frowned on in the rest.

Then, with chest heaving and muscles burning, things got worse. I became stuck. I yanked and pounded on one foot then the other, but neither would budge. I continued to moan and scream. Right up until the moment I toppled over backwards. I lay there helpless, aching, praying for relief, my limbs a frozen tangle dangling above my head.

I eventually freed myself and settled for watching the rest of the yoga show. I would have turned it off but the remote was five feet away, and I wasn't able to stand, much less walk.

The next day I slept late. But it wouldn't have mattered if I had awakened in time to see the yoga lady. I was still so sore I couldn't get out of bed. Afterwards, my early mornings were reserved for better things, like sleep.

These days just the mention of the word "lotus" sends chills down my spine. I still believe in the value of exercise, but I'm a lot more careful about how I use my body.

Love may hurt, but yoga hurts worse.

"Breakin' Up is Hard to Do," Part One
Neil Sedaka, 1962

I'll never forget that first time.

My life was perfect...the sky was always blue, the birds were always singing and my feet barely touched the ground when I walked. Then without warning, the lady in my life walked up, smiled and said, "I think we've grown apart. We're starting junior high next year, and I'm moving on to bigger and better things. See ya."

I was devastated. I begged her to reconsider. June Johnson was the first girl I'd ever kissed. The first girl I'd swapped school pictures with. The first girl I'd spent my own money on. And after only a few weeks together, she was tearing my heart out, walking away as if ours had been some childish fling, not the eternal bliss of lore and legend.

That incident with June gave me the idea of putting the breakup shoe on the other foot, but in high school I discovered that uncoupling was no less painful when I was the one pulling the plug. My senior year was looming, and after several months of teenage monogamy I decided the time had come to deliver the "We've grown apart" speech to Darlene Dawson.

I damn near died trying. I walked up to her, wheezing, coughing and sputtering, and when I finally managed to choke out the message, I felt like I had swum through a septic tank.

It didn't affect Darlene quite the same way. I believe her reaction was, "Fine, jerk. I can do better, anyway."

The next night she went out on a date. I stayed home nursing a heartache that neither Hank Williams nor Blue Ribbon could budge.

I seemed to take those early splits harder than my lady friends. I thought it was because I was a romantic, sensitive guy who had made the tragic error of dating callous, shallow chicks who didn't understand or appreciate the beauty and grandeur of true love.

That wasn't it at all. According to Todd Shackleford, I was just a victim of jealous sperm. Shackleford, an assistant professor of psychology at Florida Atlantic University, says guys pining away over lost love have nothing to do with blue moons, ebb tides or anything else so romantic. It's simply a case of evolutionary biology.

Shackleford studied 388 women and 304 men who were in "committed" relationships. His findings showed that the more time spent apart after sex, the more anxious a man became to "date" his partner again. The urge, along with the sperm count, actually increased measurably by the hour.

According to the study, men were responding to a primal evolutionary drive to keep fertilizing their female to insure that some backdoor lover didn't slip in and pollute the gene pool.

This phenomenon, known as "sperm competition," has been documented in other animals, but Shackleford's study claims to show for the first time that it exists in man.

And the key word here is "man," because the study showed a disturbing difference in women.

Apparently the female urge to copulate doesn't vary between encounters, regardless of the elapsed time. (Unless, of course, a woman is offered a new car or a trip to the Riviera, at which time the lust monkey leaps out of the closet at warp speed.) The Shackleford study says the female "heat factor" is hardwired for "sizzle," "sauté" or "defrost," and time apart from that "special man" doesn't change a thing.

Bluntly put, absence does not make the female heart grow fonder.

The theory of sperm competition may explain why some guys have a hard time saying goodbye, but no study or lecture or theory will ever explain why some guys just don't get it, why they can't seem to anticipate the damage that occurs when a relationship is ripped and torn and pulled apart.

Maybe it's because some guys just don't learn anything until they've "been there, done that." Of course, by then it's too late. Too late to understand that it only seemed hard to call it quits after you've given a girl a class ring or a friendship bracelet or even a promise.

Breaking up doesn't really get tough until you've given a girl your name.

"Breakin' Up is Hard To Do," Part Two
Neil Sedaka, 1962

From baby bottles to cups and glasses. From diapers to training pants. It's human nature to move ahead. Even in relationships.

We start with vows of friendship. When we get older, we go steady. And when going steady just isn't enough, we become engaged to be married.

Engagement is an interesting process. Centuries ago, young ladies were pledged, promised or betrothed—often at an alarmingly early age—to either an existing dude or a player to be named later (as long as he had the proper family tree or political connections).

This served two very practical purposes. First, the engagement announced to the world that a hot young lass was officially off the matrimony market. Second, it announced to a fretful peasant population that all was well because the king's Alpo-eating daughter had snagged a man and the monarchy was safe for another generation.

Modern engagements still serve two important, if slightly different, purposes. First, they allow the bride-to-be adequate time to drool over every wedding magazine in existence and plan a fairy-tale ceremony fit for a princess. Second, they allow the groom time to make a few payments on the engagement ring before saying "I do."

Engagements are festive affairs. They are announced with festive invitations, which contain the names of the victims, the time and place of the wedding, and a five-page insert listing the names of every store, from Saks Fifth Avenue to Burger King, where the happy couple has registered for bridal gifts.

The word goes out and the gifts pile up. Unfortunately, so does the stress. Between the bride fretting over fitting bunches of buddies with outlandish dresses and the groom brooding over the proper beer to serve with stamp-sized cucumber sandwiches, things can get hectic.

It makes some couples hotheaded. It leaves others cold-footed. Sometimes to the point of halting the hitching. When this happens, the unhappy couple quietly spread the word, return the gifts and, red-faced, say "No harm done" and call it quits.

It hurts but it happens. And on the bright side, when you break an engagement, all that's broken is a promise, a heart and a motel reservation or two.

But some couples survive the engagement ritual and eventually move on to marriage. Half the time, it actually works. But there's that pesky other half, those couples who after days, years or sometimes decades decide that they just can't go on being man and wife.

But this time the breaking up is a little tougher. And not just in the eyes of the law. People who marry don't just "promise" to love, cherish, honor and ignore piles of dirty laundry until death does them part. They take a vow to this effect. And they don't just make this vow to each other. God is a party to the transaction.

And while it's tough to tell your true love the thrill is gone, looking God in the face and saying "King's X, just fooling" is quite another matter.

Even in those cases where marriages should end. And those cases do exist. Some folks make great dates and lousy mates. And when abuse or deception is involved, couples are often better off apart than together. Thankfully, modern law allows for needed corrections in those instances. Unfortunately, modern law allows couples to split up over the mildest inconvenience as well.

Getting a divorce is no problem at all these days. It's as easy as picking up the phone and saying "no fault."

That's all you do. Then you simply switch your heart's ignition key to "off" and hold on tight until it's over.

Nothing to it, really.

"Walk Like a Man"
The Four Seasons, 1963

It was quite a summer for my pal Kay Coffman. When school let out she was a flat-chested, buck-toothed, shy-acting sweetheart who liked to ride bikes and listen to records with me. By Labor Day, her teeth were straight, her mouth was smeared with lipstick and her sweaters bulged with interesting new material.

It was a whole new Kay, one I was anxious to know better. But when I suggested we expand our relationship beyond repairing each other's bikes, she announced that since she was now a "woman," she would only kiss athletes.

When I reminded her I had lettered in both basketball and track at our school, she scoffed and said the only sport that mattered was football.

I was deflated...and desperate. Music was my thing. I could whip through a major scale in nothing flat and play any piece of music at one glance, but those qualities were worthless where Kay was concerned.

So I signed up to play football for the Goodwyn Junior High Warriors. The coach was Jackie Spencer. The biggest player was a guy who had failed seventh grade twice and had the build of a grizzly bear. I thought of him as Mr. Big. It was less frightening than "the dude who wants to disassemble you."

He and I had gotten acquainted the previous spring when I moved to town. On my first day at Goodwyn, he pronounced me a "smart-mouthed, four-eyed geek" and invited me to meet him after school so he could express his displeasure further.

I stupidly accepted his invitation and spent most of the afternoon with Mr. Big kneeling on my chest and leisurely beating me to a pulp.

I thought maybe that episode had gotten me out of his system, but apparently it hadn't. When Mr. Big heard I was coming out for football, he started drooling more than normal.

Since I wasn't big enough to tackle anyone, Coach Spencer made me a running back. I positively beamed. Running back! I knew Kay would be impressed.

I spent the first day of practice on the sidelines. On the second day the coach waved me in and gave me the play.

"The quarterback's gonna fake left, pivot back to the right and hand off to you. Take it through the 3-hole."

"The what?"

"The 3-hole, right between those two guys. Just run right through there."

"OK, Coach."

The quarterback took the snap and whirled. I grabbed the handoff and looked for the hole. It was gone, replaced by a churning mass of young lads, grunting in squeaky voices that hadn't completely changed and anxious to prove their manhood at my expense.

But before I could blink, the crowd parted and I saw nothing but grass between me and the end zone.

I had this view for approximately 1/100 of a second before the empty space was filled by the hulking form of Mr. Big. I ran right into him, my helmet hitting him about navel high. He carried me backwards ten yards, jumped straight up in the air and came down with a thud, right on top of me.

The blow left me seeing stars and gasping for breath. Coach Spencer was fond of saying things like "Suck it up." At 105 pounds, I didn't have much to suck up, but I did manage to finally spill my guts. All over Mr. Big.

The next day, in the interest of my personal well-being, I gave up football.

I limped for weeks. Every time Kay saw me she said, "Buzz off, creep. You walk like a sissy."

I never got that football letter. But I learned how to work the saxophone, and a few years later my rhythm and blues band played a frat party at the University of Alabama. Kay Coffman showed up with a former Alabama football player whose career had been cut short by a knee injury. The dude was so crippled up he could hardly walk.

Our band was a big hit, and Kay hinted she'd like to leave the party with me. Too late. I had already accepted an offer from another coed who just *loved* the saxophone and thought I danced "way cool."

A word to all you boys in the band. Keep blowing those horns, guys. Football fame is fleeting. A good set of lips is forever.

"Why Do Fools Fall In Love?"
Frankie Lymon & The Teenagers, 1956

Why, indeed? It's a question that's never been answered, one that's baffled the world's greatest minds, the all-time stumper in the game of human relations.

Sigmund Freud gave it a shot but didn't come close. He laid thousands of folks down on his couch in Vienna and talked dirty to them, but he got sex and love confused. In the end, he came up with some lame theory about little girls wanting to date their daddies and little boys wanting to take Daddy's place at the dinner table, even if it meant carving up Pop instead of the Christmas goose.

The poets have beaten love to death, and they've made some progress on the who, what, when and where, but the "why" still escapes them.

Even science has given it a shot. By studying everything from hormones to hairlines, the test tube types have come up with some convincing arguments about why people are attracted to one another, but even fruit flies are attracted to each other. Love is another matter entirely.

I'm no expert, but I have a theory. I think humans fall in love because they know something that a certain dog I once had didn't.

He showed up one day in the summer of '67. My roommates and I tossed him a chicken bone or a scrap of bologna, and that was enough to convince him he'd found a family.

He liked it when you rubbed his belly or scratched behind his ears or talked sweetly to him. My roommates wouldn't let him in the house, but when they were out, I'd sneak him inside and we'd watch a ball game on TV or listen to records.

He was the best three-legged dog I ever saw.

Tripod never caught the cars he limped after and he never danced a jig on his single hind leg, but he seemed as happy as a dog can be. As far as he knew, life was complete.

But humans are different. Humans know something's missing. We can work and play and eat and sleep and function just fine, but we still know there's something missing. Until we've been in love, we don't know what it is.

We're all born with a hole inside us. It's deep and dark and it nags and itches and screams for attention. We try to fill it with sex or drugs or money or anything else we can get our hands on, but those things don't work.

The hole in humans can't be filled with bright lights or brown whiskey. It can only be filled with someone else. And not just anyone, but a special someone with the power to calm our fears, give us hope, and smooth the wrinkles out of our soul.

Once we meet that person, our view of the world is forever changed.

When you're in love the sky is always blue, the beer is always cold and the jokes are always funny.

When you're in love, just holding hands can make you break a sweat. Love transforms the act of reproduction from an aerobic exercise into a communion of souls.

And love isn't just blind but deaf and dumb as well. Love overlooks dirty laundry and runny noses. Love excuses rude noises and short tempers. Love turns major aggravations into fleabites.

That's what love does. It hurts and it's messy and sometimes it's fleeting and sometimes it's forever, but anyone who's had a taste always goes back for seconds.

And that's why fools fall in love. And why they always will. Again and again and again. Because love does something to us that nothing else can.

Love makes us whole.

And if you're a human, that's as good as it gets.

"Wishin' and Hopin'"
Dusty Springfield, 1964

Time changes many things, most notably our desires.

I can't remember the grade, maybe third or fourth, but I remember having a single wish that burned so brightly as to obliterate all other thoughts. I wanted to ride in Ray Bloch's flying saucer.

He promised me he had one. He described the trips he took in it. He said over and over that soon, he'd pick me up and we'd go for a spin. I bugged him until he finally named a day.

The night before, I hardly slept. The next day, school took forever and I raced home, changed into a warm jacket and stood in the yard to wait for Ray and his saucer to arrive.

I stood there until the sun went down and supper got cold. I stood there until the cicadas quit singing. I stood there until the dew began to soak my shoes. My mother finally came outside and gently told me the wait was over. She was nice enough not to say, "I told you so."

That one stung so bad I didn't wish for anything again until the tenth grade when I saw Marilyn Hartshaw in a low-cut dress and immediately started praying for a hot, steamy session in the backseat of a '59 Cadillac.

Might as well have been wishing for another flying saucer ride.

The date was a bust, but it did fire up the wishing machine again, and I got busy. All during high school I wished like a madman, but somehow things never turned out quite right. I don't know whether I wasn't stating my desires clearly enough or had a bad wishing mechanism, but I was certainly not getting the results I wanted.

For instance, I went through a phase when I wanted to be a rock star. I envisioned myself on stage in spangled suits, with thousands of girls screaming my name. Instead of making the cover of *Rolling Stone*, I wound up being selected for the high school All-State band. When's the last time you heard of a bassoon groupie?

In college, after a friend came back to school raving about his summer in Italy, I vowed to travel the world. A few months later I wound up riding a Greyhound bus from Atlanta to Augusta so the love of my life could inform me I was being dumped. Not quite the trip I'd dreamed of.

A few years later I read some books about a detective who was also a gourmet chef, and I vowed to sample some of the same delectable dishes he described in the books. When I was invited to a chitlin supper in Opp, Alabama, I figured my gourmet days had passed me by.

Of course, a few came true. When both my kids were born, I wished as hard as I could that they'd grow up healthy and happy, and so far that one's working out fine. I never wished for good pets but got them anyway, and that's a pretty nice bonus. And I finally got to do a little traveling, so I can check that one off the list.

For the past few years, I've cut back on the wishes, figuring there wasn't much point at my age. But I realized maybe it wasn't too late to get it right if I'd just make the wishes sensible enough.

I'm giving it one more shot.

It's too late to wish for perfect health, but I'm gonna hope like crazy that I can make it the next 20 or so years without being plagued by the heartbreak of uncontrollable flatulence. In the music category, I don't want to rock the arenas anymore, but I don't think it's too much to ask that the hearing holds out as long as the desire to listen.

As for air travel, I'll simply hope that my luggage arrives at the same time and the same place as I do.

And finally, in the vanity category...I used to want one of those knock-'em-dead Hollywood smiles. These days, I'm just hoping to keep the teeth.

"Young Girl"
Gary Puckett & The Union Gap, 1968

You live a few years, you hear it plenty of times, from parents, preachers, friends. Older guy, younger girl, strictly taboo. Especially with a girl this young. I knew the rule, but it was one I couldn't follow. Not with her. Our relationship could have been a recipe for trouble, but I didn't care.

I'd known her since she arrived in town. We'd hung out a little, even managed a few weekend drives (in broad daylight), but her mother was always hovering, always watching, ready to pounce if I made a wrong move.

The "quality time" I craved was hard to come by. It was a scheduling problem. I spent my days at a school that she didn't attend. After school I was always fooling around with the kids in the band, sometimes until too late to contact her. I knew it was mostly my fault, but still, not seeing her drove me crazy, and I vowed I wouldn't rest until I had one night alone with her.

That night finally came, but it began more like a nightmare than a dream.

Her mother was out of town, and so was mine. I was excited, but my hopes for a hot evening cooled when I learned my sweetie was sick. She was new in town and hadn't made any friends she could call for help. Aside from her mother, I was the only person she could trust to take care of her, and when she called out, I rushed to her side.

I could see she was in pain. Wave after wave of cramps wrenched her abdomen, leaving her gasping and choking as the tears streamed down her face.

It hurt just to watch, and I thought about calling a doctor but decided to wait, to hold her and try to comfort her myself.

I brought her cool drinks and rubbed her face with a wet cloth, and when the pains grew worse, I held her close and stroked her head and whispered that everything would be all right. She was too sick to talk back, but that didn't stop me. I babbled on alone, cooing in that romantic gibberish that only the truly smitten can speak or understand.

When she was quiet, I held her and marveled at the simple rhythm of her heart beating against my chest. It was a moment of pure joy...and sheer terror. I had an angel in my arms, but I knew if I messed things up and her mother found out, I was dead.

Sometime after midnight I clicked off the TV, put some soft music on the stereo and asked her to dance. When she didn't object, I took her in my arms and began to move gently, careful not to hurt her. She clung to me as if she were afraid she might fall off the edge of the earth. I clutched her back, and cheek to cheek we spun slowly around the floor. Those few minutes seemed like hours.

When we sat down again, she fell asleep in my arms, exhausted from the pain and the late hour. I never dozed, never moved, afraid I might break the magic spell. The rest of the night passed in silence, and when the sun rose, she stirred and yawned, and I looked down at her.

The pain was gone, and she looked around and blinked, slowly coming awake. She stretched once, twice, again. Then she looked me right in the face, and the little pout on her lips blossomed into a gorgeous toothless grin as her diaper filled up and overflowed all over my lap.

My daughter continued to have tummy trouble until she was almost a year old, and we spent many more nights in the rocking chair, waiting for the pain to pass and the sun to rise. They were all memorable, but that first night alone together is the one I'll never forget.

"D-I-V-O-R-C-E"
Tammy Wynette, 1968

A couple of couples I know are about to have babies. Gifts are in order, and while I haven't made a purchase yet, I have peeked at the current crop of "baby books."

They're filled with colorful drawings and clever poems and special spots to post notes and photos about "Baby's First Step" or "Baby's First Tooth" or "Baby's First Mutual Fund."

I was relieved to see the bookstores still don't have a space for "Baby's First Divorce." But the way things are going in modern America, they soon may. With marriages failing at a rate of almost fifty percent, divorce these days isn't so much a long shot as an odds-on bet for newlyweds.

I'm old enough to remember when it wasn't that way. When Ozzie and Harriet and Beaver Cleaver were American role models, divorce was still a major social taboo. From elementary through high school, I only knew one kid whose parents were divorced. It simply wasn't done. It wasn't even talked about.

But what was barely mentioned in polite circles forty years ago is now advertised on billboards and late-night TV. At the end of the nineties, divorce is more socially acceptable than deer hunting.

Perhaps that's why more and more people choose divorce. That, and the fact that you can now get divorced for just about any reason under the sun. In ancient times couples were rarely granted a split unless infidelity or infertility were involved. These days, the motive can be as vague as "incompatibility" or as trivial as "inconvenience."

But while divorce is easily granted, it is not easily endured. At least not for anyone who still gives half a damn about a person they once thought enough of to promise to stick with until separated by six feet of dirt.

People talk about "good divorces." Maybe some are better than others, but none are "good." Divorce is an ugly, brutal business. It rips and tears and scars, not on the outside, but deep down where the hurt doesn't show and the healing can take forever. Especially when children are involved.

And then there are the questions...so many, and so bad. Relationships are filled with questions from day one, but never so much as when the needle starts drifting towards "E" on the love gauge.

Couples question everything...their dedication, their willpower, their faith, their very sanity. They reach for everything from Jack Daniels to Jesus in search of an answer.

But the reasons for most divorces aren't printed in black and white. Too often, they're gray, ghostly phantoms drifting through a clouded field of once-bright memories.

And when painful personal questions arise, it's natural to want to assign blame. Sometimes, it's not that hard. People lie, people cheat, people beat. In those instances it may be easy to point to an act or a person and say that's why this must end.

But while divorce is sometimes justified, it should never be glorified. Despite the bad jokes about cranky ex-husbands and flaky ex-wives, any marriage that ends without a sense of loss was not a marriage to begin with but merely a date done to excess.

There's an ugly truth about divorce that seldom gets mentioned. Despite the hype and the spin in the feel-good nineties, divorce doesn't liberate or illuminate. It destroys hopes and crumbles dreams and tears families apart.

Every divorce begins with a thousand questions. But after the shouting has stopped and the papers are filed, only one remains.

Only one, but it's the cruelest question of all...

"What's wrong with me?"

"Return to Sender"
Elvis Presley, 1962

When the Greyhound from Augusta dropped me off in Atlanta, the clock read 2 a.m., the thermometer 8 degrees. It was a bad Sunday morning. It would be a worse Tuesday. That's when the last letter would arrive from the girl I'd just spent the day with, the one I'd been head-over-heels in love with for the past year.

Being dumped via U.S. Mail might seem cold, but in this case it was appropriate. Our relationship had been mostly postal.

We met on a blind date but became well enough acquainted during a drive-in double feature to know we wanted seconds. Unfortunately, the next day she was back off to her college, I to mine.

Separated by 500 miles, without a car between us, cozy weekends were out. The phone was too expensive, but stamps were a nickel a pop and we wore out the mail routes between Atlanta and Oxford, Mississippi.

I wrote her every day, sometimes twice. And every day, I'd get a letter back. My dorm room was right across the parking lot from the post office, and I wore a rut in the asphalt going back and forth to check my cubby for another of her sweetly scented love notes.

Looking back, the mail was probably the safest place for our relationship to develop. In our letters we were funny, charming, thoughtful, romantic, caring. Face-to-face, we were like a pair of minks on date night. Our infrequent weekend visits weren't so much romantic interludes as extended conjugal visits, minus the main dish.

If we had been together too often, we would probably have been reduced to ash by the sheer heat of our physical relationship.

These days it seems pretty shallow to base a relationship solely on lust. Luckily, I didn't have a problem with it then. And it's not like we didn't talk at all. We breathed every now and then.

It was like that for over a year. And then came that cold February when she got sick and went home to Augusta. It wasn't a major problem but enough to require an overnight hospital stay. Naturally I was on the first bus out, determined to be by her side, panting and drooling when she awakened.

Unfortunately, I wasn't the only drooler in the joint.

The hospital also housed her former boyfriend, an up-and-coming orderly. I learned this from her mother as we paced the waiting room together. When she emerged from surgery whole and healthy, I sneaked a kiss, groped a few unbandaged areas and headed back to Atlanta.

Two days later, the letter came. I knew it was trouble when the envelope smelled like rubbing alcohol instead of Chanel. She said she was going back to the old flame. That he was gonna work his way up from bedpans and become a doctor, sweeping her along in the process. She wished me well. I honestly can't remember if I wrote back, although it would have been in character to do some begging.

So we broke up. The letter has vanished, but not the memories. Not a one.

I hope her dreams came true. I hope she's Mrs. Doctor Somebody now. In fact I hope her guy is a heart specialist. And if so, next time I need some work done on the ticker I may ask for a freebie from the guy who put the first crack in my heart to begin with.

Of course if he can't do it for free, he could charge a small amount. But I hope he'll fax the bill. Or phone it in. It's been a while, but I'm still not ready for another piece of medically scented mail from Augusta.

"Wouldn't It Be Nice"
The Beach Boys, 1966

Once upon a time, the Beach Boys complained in song about having to wait until they were older to get married and have sex. Older? Wait? Dust off the dinosaurs, professor. Clear some shelf space in the museum of popular culture. The thoughts expressed in this hit song are already fossilized.

When they released this 1966 smash, the Beach Boys were singing about sex. About not having it. For the majority of young people, premarital sex was a major societal taboo. In those seemingly innocent times, it just wasn't fashionable for a young man to test-drive his future wife.

It certainly wasn't a consideration for me. I was chaste, but not by choice. I had the same urges as everyone else, but even my best romantic efforts failed to bear fruit. I heard the stories, the rumors about certain girls at school who "put out," but those young ladies were most definitely beyond my reach.

Girls like that didn't waste their charms on four-eyed, 140-pound, bassoon-playing geeks. They reserved themselves for the high school's upper crust, the "popular" boys. But even though my pleas for pleasure went unheard or unheeded, and even though I thought of little else, I admit to having some qualms. Even as my body was consumed with the fires of lust, my mind was ablaze with images of fire and brimstone and pitchfork-wielding people in red suits.

I knew if I ever so much as glimpsed a bit of naked female flesh, it would be tattooed with an image of Satan saying "Gotcha!"

It was a predictable result of my upbringing. I was raised in a devout Southern Baptist household and spent countless days and nights listening to lurid pulpit warnings about the perils of young lust. In a bit of unfortunate timing, I reached high school at the same time as my preacher's two daughters. As a result, he spent increasingly more time railing against the evils of teenage lust.

My mother, the church secretary, spent a great deal of time reiterating the reverend's ramblings. Between mother and the preacher, I felt like the filling in a sin sandwich.

Looking back, it was probably for the best. If by some miracle I had actually scored in those days, the guilt would have been unbearable. I'm convinced I would have felt compelled to abandon my carnal ways and take up missionary work in the Congo to expunge my grievous errors.

In high school the closest I came to glory land was a brief stop at third base. My visit at that long-sought location ended abruptly when the young lady in question issued the standard sexual ultimatum of the day.

Marriage. That was the ticket. The unwritten rule for most kids my age was, if you wanted sex, you got married. Period. Paragraph. End of story. A "nice" girl didn't say "I will" until the boy said "I do."

But as soon as I graduated from high school, everything changed. It seemed as if overnight the world had tilted on its sexual axis. The cultural revolution of the '60s was starting to hit its stride. Civil rights protesters were bleeding in the streets. The women's movement found its voice, and a popular form of social expression was having sex. Whenever, wherever and with whomever you wanted.

I was ecstatic. Surely, I thought, my time had finally come. How could it be otherwise? Every day the radio was blaring "Let's Spend The Night Together," and crowds in the streets were carrying signs saying "Make Love, Not War."

Love and War. I wouldn't learn until much later that in certain relationships, it's hard to tell the difference.

"Slow Dancin'"
Johnny Rivers, 1977

Somewhere between the first limbo and the last twist I began to fall apart. By the time the amps were unplugged I was limping badly, and the next morning I felt like I'd been massaged by a steamroller.

With marriage and kids, the dances had become fewer and farther between. While I endured the special occasions like class reunions or New Year's Eve, I was always thankful when the last record played. And on that disastrous night when the party turned painful, I knew the time had come to yield the floor to the Clearasil crowd.

The young heal quickly. They can endure, even enjoy, the noise and the sweat and the smoke of that social battlefield known as the dance floor. For them, the dance is not just a celebration of youth and life but a way of meeting, choosing, thinning the herd of potential partners.

But as the years pile up, the steps change, and the motivation. Long after you've scored your last touchdown or led your last cheer, when the hair is thinning and the Wonderbra is working overtime, dancing remains the last unbroken link with the past. For some lucky couples the musical motions are a pleasant way of keeping in touch with someone and some- *thing* held dear.

Other twosomes aren't so fortunate. After a divorce, it's usually a problem in the pairing. In dancing, as in life, the fewer partners, the better. A bad match at either can be disastrous. And even a good match can be tricky for an unfamiliar duo.

Matching old moves to a new mate involves some risk, some sacrifice. It requires a willingness to abandon the lifetime of memories attached to each tune. It means learning that the special song that meant so much with one partner will be mere noise in the arms of another. It's a tricky step, but one some couples manage to master.

But there are others who never find the right partner. Late in life and still labeled "single," they seek to correct that condition at any price.

Night after night, propped against the jukebox, they wait and listen for the call that never comes. Their search for lost hope is frantic and joyless. And when the dance floor is no longer filled with fresh faces and taut bodies but covered with bran eaters and calorie counters, it can be a grim scene.

Went there. Did that. Once was enough.

The lights are just as bright, the air just as smoky, but the loudest sound is not the roar of the music but the ticking of the clock. The odor of sweet perfume is masked by the heavy scent of desperation.

And the first dance is no longer an introduction but an offer of availability, a crude note in physical shorthand addressed to anyone willing to quiet the whispers of loneliness for just one night.

The newly paired strangers don't dip and whirl lightly. Their dance is an urgent battle with private demons, an exercise that leaves them spent and staggering, clinched like a pair of punched-out boxers at the final bell.

But they continue, hoping to find the magic in the music one last time. Sometimes they do. But even then, they move with caution, looking over a shoulder, hoping the past isn't waiting to cut in, praying that the music's end won't find them with the wrong partner.

And then the slow dance is no longer the sweetest of all, but the saddest.

Fortunately for me, the dancing days are not quite done. There's one last waltz on my schedule. One I've planned forever. One I've danced a thousand times in my dreams. A special moment with a special partner. One last whirl with a young girl in white...

A wedding dance between father and bride.

"The Game of Love"
Wayne Fontana and the Mindbenders, 1965

Love is the oldest, strangest and roughest game known to man.

Love can leave you aching in places you can't protect (at least until someone invents a pad for the heart), but some of the bumps and bruises could be avoided if people knew what to expect. The problem is, love is a game without any rules. We learn to play by trial and error.

There aren't any rules, but experience teaches us all some lessons about love. If we take them to heart, chances are good we'll play the game better each time around.

These are some of mine. If you're new at the game, try these next time you suit up. They might save you some wear and tear.

1. There's Someone For Everyone. It's true. Even Adolf Hitler had Eva Braun. But remember that Hollywood learned long ago to shoot the close-ups slightly out of focus. There's a reason. Brad Pitt has morning breath and Ashley Judd gets cranky once a month. Don't expect your "special someone" to be any different.

2. People Aren't Projects. Human beings are not slabs of raw marble waiting to be chiseled to perfection by someone else. People have flaws. If you can't learn to love them, learn to accept them. If you're a person who feels the need to change things, take up politics or interior decorating.

3. Regular Maintenance Required. You change the oil in your car. Do the same for your attitude. If you don't drain your emotional crankcase on a regular basis, you'll develop a major sludge problem. Despite what your doctor says, nothing clogs a heart faster than bad memories.

4. No Hitting. Open hands and closed fists can speak volumes, but the message is never good. No one ever beat their way to happiness. And in the same vein...No Hitting Below The Belt. Sex should be a wonder, not a weapon.

5. Cash Shouldn't Count. Don't base your love on the bottom line. If you judge a good time by the price tag, sooner or later you'll find a piece of "happiness" you just can't afford. And remember, people can make money, but money can't make people.

6. Three Is Enough. At least when it comes to "magic words." Never start a sentence with "I love you, but..."

7. Have Faith. In each other, if nothing else. Sometimes, it's the only

thing that gets you through the night.

8. Be Patient. Love is a fortress built one brick at a time, but it can be destroyed with a few harsh words. When things get rough, start counting. Count to ten. If that's not enough, try twenty, or a hundred, or even a million. Time consuming, sure, but it beats restacking all those bricks.

9. Clean Up After Yourself. This applies to everything from dirty dishes to dirty deeds. When you make a mistake, admit it, apologize and ask for forgiveness. And don't procrastinate. Unlike wine, bad news doesn't improve with age.

10. Some Assembly Required. Love is a puzzle but you don't get all the pieces at once. They're delivered over time. Treasure each one, find its special spot, and when the last piece is in place, you'll have created a thing of beauty that makes Mona Lisa look like a bad blind date.

While these suggestions may help, the game isn't played on paper. You have to get in there and mix it up. It hurts, and you'll bleed and you'll laugh and you'll cry but sooner or later, you'll get hooked. And you'll keep playing. We all do, because it's still the greatest game going.

And there's a big difference between this game and all the others. If you play the game of love just right...nobody loses.

ANIMALS, VEGETABLES, MINERALS AND MISCELLANEOUS STUFF

It's hard to gather all your thoughts under a single umbrella. Here's a collection of unconnected thoughts about unconnected things. This made sense to me. Your mileage— and tolerance—may vary.

Dad's Doubts About Down Under

Every few years my grown-up baby girl, Heather, gets an irresistible urge to see the world. The last time this condition popped up she spent three months in Europe.

This time it's a shorter trip—two months—but a longer plane flight… all the way to Australia.

Since she's planned and saved and taken care of things like keeping her health insurance in force, I can't complain. And when she mentioned Australia, I was actually relieved.

Everything I'd ever heard about the Land Down Under was positive: pretty scenery, nice people, English language and good national math skills.

Australia hadn't even had a terrorist attack. It seemed like a good choice.

Then Heather gave me her "Let's Go" travel guide to Australia.

"Read this, Dad," she said. "You'll see how much fun it's going to be."

The first part of the book, about currency exchange and where to get stitched up after a rugby riot, didn't interest me. I went straight to the section titled "The Great Outdoors."

The first few paragraphs raved about Australia's glorious beaches, snow-capped mountains and delightful deserts. It sounded like the word Australia could mean "God's Rough Draft of Heaven." When I got to the second page, I realized the word "Australia" actually means "Place of Sudden, Unexpected Violent Death."

I got my first clue from the headline that said "Dangerous Animals."

When I think about Australian critters, I envision cute kangaroos and cuddly koalas. The guidebook might have mentioned those, but I didn't get that far. I started choking in the first paragraph, which contained this nugget: "Australia is home to the world's most poisonous snakes." It went on to mention them all, and how long it took to die from each one's bite.

Also mentioned was the redback spider, which "can cause serious illness and death."

The beach isn't much better. And the problem isn't the notorious great white shark. The problem is the box jellyfish, whose "stings can be fatal even after they are washed ashore." Stings are so common the beaches are stocked with containers full of vinegar, which jellyfish victims can rub on the bite to reduce the swelling while they await transportation to the emergency room. Or the morgue.

If you're in a boat, things aren't much better. Especially if you come across saltwater crocodiles, which the Aussies call "snapping handbags."

It's probably coincidence that the day after I read about the croc in the tourist guide, I came across an article in the *Times* of London headlined "Killer Croc Attacks Canoe Pair."

The story was from Australia. It said in part, "Barry Jeffries, 60, was pulled into the water as the crocodile lunged at him as he attempted to fight it off with an oar. His wife, Glenda, swam ashore to safety, but rescuers searching the Normanby River on the remote Cape York in far north Queensland have yet to find his body."

Great. I thought about asking my daughter to find a nice, safe hotel in the heart of Sydney and stay there until I say it's safe to come home. Then I remembered that last week I sent her an article about a man attacking Sydney hotel guests with a tomahawk and a machete.

I'm probably concerned about nothing. She'll probably be fine. And besides, she starts her trip with three weeks in New Zealand. According to tourist websites, New Zealand has no poisonous snakes and only one deadly spider. It came from Australia.

She's a smart girl and knows how to take care of herself, so I know I shouldn't be worried. But I'm her daddy, too. Which is why, while she's shopping for adventure gear, I'm checking the Sydney yellow pages to see where she can buy bug spray and bazookas.

A dad can't be too careful these days.

Southern Tradition Endangered

If Satan has children, they must look like this.

I spotted the creature along a well-traveled stretch of highway just outside a town too small for a stoplight. I'd heard they were here, but I'd also heard that the moon landing was fake and pro wrestling was real, so I decided to play it safe and check it out for myself.

I stopped the car, got out...and began to tremble.

Gray and gritty, covered with armor plating, sporting a long snout and spiky tail, there it was...a full-grown, nine-banded armadillo, not five miles from my front door.

I was horrified. Not by the creature itself. I'd encountered plenty of them while growing up in south Louisiana, and armadillos are now so common in Florida that high schools are adopting them as team mascots. I knew they existed. What scared me was the realization that they'd migrated this far north.

Since these South American imports obviously didn't come here in search of higher-paying jobs or better schools, there seemed to be just one explanation—global warming.

In the past it was a phenomenon I hadn't worried about. Even if global warming believers are correct and the world is headed for a permanent rise in temperature, the only downside so far seems to be the possibility of an actual summer in Siberia and a longer soybean season in South Dakota. Hardly cause for alarm.

And if a few icebergs melt and a few million beachfront condos slip beneath the surf, it's no skin off my nose. Besides, it's real estate. It's risky.

I figure we can deal with the weather-related effects of global warming. I'm less sure about our reaction to the cultural consequences. Consequences I hadn't considered until I came across the armadillo resting on the roadside.

These things are bad news for several reasons. For one, because they eat insects, which is not bad in itself, but the insects armadillos love best live beneath the earth. To get at them, armadillos use their sharp little claws to go through dirt faster than politicians go through money.

And they don't care if the soil they disturb happens to cover your yard, your garden or your golf course. But sod can be patched. What can't be is a great Southern tradition.

Possums have long been praised in Southern song, dance and literature, but they have a definite downside. Since they are slow, not to mention stupid, many of them wind up as the decoration of choice for Southern road shoulders. Books of roadkill recipes (and there are several) invariably feature possum as the pièce de résistance.

And now this Southern cultural icon is threatened by a south-of-the-border bandit. It ain't right.

We're all fired up about saving the whales. How about protecting the possum? If there's any justice in this world, a program will soon be created to preserve this marvelous marsupial and restore it to its rightful place in the ecosystem...beneath a set of tires.

Not quite three years ago, billions of people panicked at the specter of something called Y2K. It was a computer problem that was predicted to cause planes to fall from the sky, power plants to shut down and the earth to spin off its axis all because a bunch of computers couldn't figure out how to count to 2,000. It never happened, but the mere thought of Y2K had millions screaming "The End Is Near."

This week Walter Cronkite said if we attack Iraq, it will trigger World War III and bring human civilization to the end of the road.

Frankly, it looks like it's too late to worry. If armadillos are already in North Georgia, the end isn't near...it's here.

And it's pretty doggone ugly.

Fast-track Weight Loss Program

Great news for folks like me! Just in time for swimsuit season, the newest fad diet has arrived. And this one might actually work.

Best of all, it's cheap. No special formulas, no prepackaged meals, no meetings, no calorie-counter cards to lug around. On this diet, all you have to do to succeed is keep your mouth shut.

Especially when you're hungry. You see, the new diet fad is that oldest method of weight control...fasting. Yes, fasting. After zillions of years of human existence, scientists have finally figured out that if you don't eat, you lose weight. OK, so maybe it's not quite that simple, but early results from a study by the National Institute on Aging look promising.

In fact, they look great.

Researchers compared results between a group given a diet that was reduced by 40 percent of normal food intake and a group that fasted every other day. The findings surprised everyone. While the reduced-calorie group lost the most weight, the every-other-day fasters showed benefits not achieved by the regular dieters, including an increased sensitivity to insulin and a marked decrease in toxins associated with brain damage in Alzheimer's patients.

Frankly, this is fabulous news for me. Looks like if I just eat every other day, the insulin shots will be history, and with any luck, I might one day remember who I took to the senior prom.

And the eating-every-other-day method may not be as big a problem as some people think. Mostly because on the days they were allowed to eat, study subjects were allowed to eat as much as they wanted.

They could absolutely pig out and the results didn't change one bit. In fact one group even had good results doing the fast over a 24-hour period of eating and abstaining. They were given the equivalent of three balanced meals and made to eat all the food in four hours. Then they fasted for twenty hours. Same results.

Although I'm pleased with the results of the study, I have to admit I'm also a bit surprised. Fasting has been the national sport of Ethiopia for years, and those folks don't exactly look like the picture of health. But then maybe they're overdoing things. And history shows that some fasters do fine. The best example is probably Mohandas Gandhi, aka Mahatma, who was a regular faster and did so well he almost single-handedly managed to kick the English out of India.

Gandhi swore by fasting, said it cleansed his mind and body and made him a much better person. And fashionably thin, I might add. In fact, if he'd lost a few more pounds, that assassin's bullets might have missed him altogether. But still, he went out with a clean spleen and unclogged arteries.

If it was good enough for Gandhi, guess it's good enough for me.

I think I'll start tomorrow when they have all-you-can-eat night at Ed's House of Fried Food and Chamber Music. I'll bloat myself to the strains of Bach and wake up the next day ready to stare starvation in the face.

Of course, I do have one teeny reservation about the study. The fact that none of the subjects have come forward to speak publicly about the experience. Mostly because they can't talk. Because they're mice. Human tests are still a year or two off. But then so what? Nothing ventured nothing gained or, in this case, lost.

Just because this program has so far been confined to rodents shouldn't keep me from giving it a go. So I'm gonna do it. What's the worst that can happen? I develop a craving for cheese? Where my health is concerned, that's one chance I'm willing to take.

He Leadeth Me Beside...

It's not every day I think about the 23rd Psalm. But a recent trip to the office restroom left me longing for some "still waters."

It was early and I had the building to myself. Before long, nature called and I headed for the men's room. These visits are usually routine, but this time, something was different.

I've been around long enough to know that from time to time the ball, or flap or some other piece of toilet intestine will go belly up, causing the toilet to run continuously. We've all had the problem, which is usually solved by (a) "jiggling" the toilet handle or (b) buying a new house.

But that fateful morning, the toilet was making a new noise. One I'd never heard before.

From outside the stall, it sounded like Niagara Falls on steroids. When I opened the door, it looked even worse.

As mentioned earlier, I prefer my toilet water still, not shaken like a James Bond martini. And this water wasn't just shaking. It was roiling, boiling, erupting in huge, gassy bubbles. As I watched, the noise grew worse, yowling, howling and roaring like the space shuttle on takeoff.

Old-timers called early toilets "thunder jars." Now I know why. But this was no antique.

As late as the early 1990s, we still had real toilets in America, man-sized monsters that could swallow up small animals and even children if given the chance. Then, the folks in charge of saving the environment declared we'd save gazillions of gallons of precious water if we started using so-called low-flow models. The law was changed, and we're now a low-flow nation. (Even though we flush twice as often to get the job done.)

This toilet was a relatively modern model, with all the new, politically correct features. And it wasn't happy. I won't claim a bathroom fixture has a life of its own. But this toilet certainly had issues. And I didn't want them to become mine.

I wasn't sure what was down there causing all the commode commotion, but I knew this: there are more things lurking in the sewers of America than most of us like to admit. The horror stories about giant alligators, man-eating possums and "missing" Mafia bosses roaming the underground tunnels of Manhattan are real.

I myself once had an across-the-street neighbor who had a close (toilet) encounter of the worst kind. One day she came running out of the house, shivering, shaking and frightened half out of her wits because something had shown up unexpectedly in her toilet. She said she was just sitting there minding her own business when—all of a sudden—she felt a nudge and took a look and almost fainted.

From her description it could have been anything from a raccoon to a Shetland pony. She asked me to come look. I asked her to take a Polaroid.

Since then I've seen countless stories about snakes slithering out of toilets, not to mention rats the size of cats. Toilets have been reported to explode and accused of being possessed by Satan.

I have yet to hear of anything good crawling out of a toilet. And if something was coming out of this one, I didn't want to be around to say hello. It's hard for a grown man to admit he's spooked by a piece of plumbing, but I was. So I did the manly thing.

I backed away, turned out the lights and left the restroom. Later that day, after several colleagues had used the toilet and returned in one piece, I went back for a look.

The still waters had returned, for which I was grateful.

But I was even more grateful that, for the time being, my urge to use the john had disappeared. I'll go back one day. But right now, where the toilet is concerned, my motto is, "There's no place like home."

Yellow Peril

On every corner the dogwoods are shaking out their pink and white cloaks as azaleas overflow their beds like crimson and white throw rugs and swollen buds pop like champagne corks on New Year's Eve.

Everywhere nature is abloom as millions of plants wipe a winter's worth of sleep from their beady little green eyes. It's an absolutely gorgeous sight. But there's a small problem. Whoever penned the line about looking good and feeling bad must have had spring in mind.

Pass the Poulan, please. I'm ready to weedeat all these oversexed green monsters right back to where they came from.

I've simply had enough. If my head were a septic tank, I'd be on speed dial to Roto-Rooter. If my sinuses were a bank account, I'd be overdrawn.

I spent enough time behind the barn to know all about the birds and the bees. And I know God made every living thing ready, willing and able to reproduce, but for my money, these plants are way out of line. I wish they'd keep their nasty business to themselves and let me breathe in peace. But no, they have to show off, do it in public and not only that, but make a mess at the same time. Everywhere you look, there's a nasty yellow cloud of goo, pouring out of plants like brimstone fumes from the very depths of hell.

When I pollinate I do it in the privacy of my own home. These plants have no more modesty than those spider monkeys on the Discovery Channel's mating special.

I don't object to consensual adult hanky-panky, but when my nostrils' rights are breached, it's time for these floral fornicators to zip it up.

And there's absolutely no way to fight back. The pollen is mostly so tiny you can't even see it coming in time to duck. It's impossible to escape this yellow peril. I keep the windows up on my car but still find telltale traces of plant petting on my dashboard. I don't get it. Why would a batch of lustful pollen violate my vehicle? To attack my radio and impregnate Dr. Laura? To knock up that nasturtium nestled in the trunk? It's ridiculous. I feel like my car's running an escort service for oversexed oleanders.

It's no better at home. You can caulk yourself silly, seal every window and duct tape the door jambs but still wake up the next day to find everything you own covered with plant sperm. It's disgusting.

What's worse, some people actually encourage this behavior. You see them each winter, skulking around their flower beds, fertilizing and pruning, probably even showing little dirty movies. Doing everything they can to encourage this vile behavior.

I say forget the Miracle-Gro. Ban the Vigoro. Give me some Vigor-Oh No. Or better yet, plaster every bed of begonias with naked pictures of Tipper Gore. That should be enough to keep anything from wanting to mate.

Meanwhile, I'm searching for remedies. So far I'm out of luck. I've taken every allergy medicine known to man and some that aren't. Forget it. They either don't work or they put you to sleep.

Well, I've made up my mind. If something's gonna be put to sleep, it's not going to be me. I say give me breath or give me death. I'll suffer through one more year of choking and wheezing and watering, but after that, no mercy.

You plants be warned. All you lustful lilies and carnal caladiums and hot-to-trot hickories. As long as there's Roundup on the shelves there's gonna be a rumble. Next winter while you're all sleeping, I'll be taking care of business.

This time next year, Old Yeller's gonna croak for good.

Johnny Appleseed was fine in his day, but right now I'm thinking it might be time for a visit from Chuckie Chainsaw.

Paving, Pennsylvania Style

I swore I'd swear off picking on this particular crowd for a while.

Time's up. I admit we Southerners make an occasional mistake. We commit the occasional faux pas. We even make the occasional screwup. What we do not do is make a mockery of common sense. In this regard, you Yankees stand head and shoulders above the rest of the world, and now you've gone and done something I cannot overlook.

Let's put it in Olympic terms. When it comes to stupid, you folks win the gold medal hands down.

This is not a random accusation. I could make that any day about a group of people who insist on defiling their grits with milk and sugar. This latest transgression also falls in the food category, but this one really takes the cake. Or I should say, the hindquarters.

The matter involves the noble deer, cherished in Southern lore and legend. We Southerners like our deer and do lots of things with them. We photograph them for their majestic beauty. We curse them for going through our vegetable gardens like four-legged dispose-alls. We kill them for food and fun.

However, there is one thing you will never see a Southerner do to a deer.

And that is, take a load of asphalt and pave over it.

Which is exactly what happened recently in Pennsylvania. According to Associated Press reports, a road crew paving a stretch of Highway 895 near the lovely hamlet of Bowmanstown decided a little organic matter never hurt things, and upon finding a deer obstructing their progress, simply paved over it rather than removing the unfortunate, and extremely dead, creature from the roadside.

In all fairness I should point out this is probably just an honest mistake on the part of the paving company. I say this after Walter Bortree, engineer in charge of the operation, explained Pennsylvania's common sense approach to highway matters by firmly declaring, "It is against state policy to pave over a deer."

I have a question. Why would a sovereign state need a policy declaring it illegal to pave over a deer? Wouldn't common sense dictate that? Or could there be a teaching problem at the state's heavy construction academies?

"Class, this here is a road bed. What you do is scrape it flat, lay down some crushed rock and top the whole thing off with a few inches of asphalt. This will make you a good, tough turnpike for years to come.

"And if you come up on a deer in your way, it's best not to pave over it. But I know schedules can get tight. Now a doe ain't much trouble, but if you get a buck with a decent rack, make sure you steamroll that sucker a time or two to get them antlers mashed down good. And if you can wait a few weeks, the job gets easier because by then they unbloat and tend to flatten out some."

Pennsylvania officials have tried to cover for the road crew, claiming they probably "just didn't see it since it was on the side of the road." The mayor of Bowmanstown disputes this, saying, "It's been there three weeks. You can't miss it. It's on a straightaway."

Let's give the crew the benefit of the doubt and say they "just didn't see it."

At least the part they paved over. As I understand it, the bottom half of the deer is still hanging out from under the pavement, lying there like the filling from an asphalt Twinkie.

I'll even go the extra mile and say the problem wasn't caused by a lack of horse sense. That it was just an exercise in the time-honored Yankee tradition of covering up problems with heavy doses of dirt. A practice commonly referred to as the Jimmy Hoffa solution.

I try and I try not to make fun of you poor, benighted Yankees. But you have to agree that when you make a boner like this, it's pretty hard to pass up.

Celebrating a New Arrival

I wanted to pass out cigars but couldn't find any with labels that said, "It's A Tomato!"

Granted, it's not much of a tomato yet. In fact, it looks more like a pregnant green pea. But since it's growing on my tomato vine, I figure it's a tomato. And I'm out to party.

I hadn't planted a garden in 20 years. The last one was a dismal failure. This year, for no particular reason, I decided to give my thumb one more shot at being green.

I went small, burying two tomatoes in a 20-gallon plastic tub. I watered and fertilized and waited, expecting the worst. After two days, the plants were still alive. After a week, they were getting bigger.

For the next month I hovered and hoped, expecting my plants to perish at any minute. Instead, they flourished. A few blooms appeared, then more, and the other day, when I went out to chase off the rabbit, there he was...Eddie Ray.

That's what I call my tomato. I know it's dumb to name a plant, but I was so excited I couldn't help it.

Eddie Ray gets cuter by the day, but plant parenthood has brought some unexpected challenges.

Once my kids were grown and gone, I thought my days as a father figure were over. But when Eddie Ray appeared, the old paternal instincts came flooding back, along with the usual hopes and fears one encounters when raising a child. Even one whose mama is a plant.

I hope Eddie Ray will grow tall and strong and be happy and enjoy a life free of nuclear war or a Hillary Clinton presidency. I can't control those things, but I'm doing all I can to make Eddie Ray as happy as the next tomato.

Luckily, it won't be expensive. I won't have to worry about having Eddie Ray's teeth bleached or buying car insurance or saving for his college education. I won't even have to give him the dreaded lecture about the "birds and the bees."

I figure my biggest problem with Eddie Ray will be deciding when to kill him and how to eat him.

As for the when, the Lord will have the final word about Eddie Ray's Judgment Day. My tomato will be ready when he's ready, and no amount of fertilizer, coaxing or pleading will hasten his march to maturity.

I don't plan to dine on a juvenile Eddie Ray. I'm gonna pick that boy at the peak of ripeness, at the top of his game, when he's oozing from every little pore, on the verge of exploding from an overload of delicious ruby-red juice.

Eating him is another matter. I haven't grown my own food in 20 years and want to make sure I get the best possible use out of Eddie Ray and his siblings, whom I expect to see any day.

I've been telling myself the first tomato was destined to be slathered in mayonnaise, salted and peppered and slid between two slices of white bread. A tomato sandwich is definitely first on the feast list, but I don't plan to sacrifice Eddie Ray entirely on the altar of Wonder Bread.

Good-sized chunks will be saved for a salad. A sliver or two will serve as a nice garnish for my sensational ground turkey surprise. With any luck I'll have enough left for tomato aspic, tomato sauce and tomato-flavored tortillas.

I've tossed out tomato scraps before, but not this time. I owe it to Eddie Ray not to demean his memory by sending his leftovers to the landfill.

And not just because it's the respectful thing to do. It's a matter of economics, too. Considering what I spent to get this boy hatched, I know for a fact that...a tomato is a terrible thing to waste.

SCIENCE, SCIENCE FICTION AND HOME IMPROVEMENTS

I like scientific discoveries and science fiction so much because I don't understand the science part and I don't believe the fiction. It's a great match. I feel the same way about appliances and roof leaks.

Smiling Swine

I've always liked science when it's answering the big questions, solving the great mysteries. I want the test tube crowd hard at work when it comes to knowing whether there's life on other planets, or if Frank and Kathie Lee will get back together, or how much wood a woodchuck could chuck.

I also cheer science's humanitarian applications, such as the cure for polio, hemorrhoid relief medications and the invention of cat litter.

Used properly, it's wonderful, but I think folks can overdo this science thing. I think it's happening now in the fertile fields of Iowa, where a lone scientist, instead of looking for a cure for cancer, is trying to discover what makes a hog happy.

Meet Hongwei Xin, a Chinese dude dedicated to creating generations of smiling swine.

For my money, sciencing a pig makes as much sense as wallpapering the inside of your toilet tank. A hog is a hog. I always thought if it had plenty of food and a nice-sized mud hole, it was happy enough. Apparently not. At least according to the Iowa Pork Producers, who are funding Xin's research.

Those Iowans want their hogs to be happy, because a happy hog is a fat hog and a fat hog is a moneymaker.

It's a temperature thing. When pigs are too cold, they shiver and burn up calories they could be using to make bacon and lard. When they're too hot, they're listless and don't eat enough to get really fat.

For a pig to be most productive, it has to be just like Goldilocks' porridge...not too hot, not too cold, but just right.

The question was, how to get it that way. For years, farmers have played hunt-and-peck with pigpen thermostats, raising and lowering them all day to try and keep their brood pleased. But they never knew if they were getting it right, because the hogs couldn't tell them.

Now they can, thanks to Xin's scientific efforts. Using computers, Xin studied pigs "at rest" to determine when they're most comfy. "At rest," by the way, means the pigs aren't eating or having sex or watching SportsCenter on ESPN but just standing still.

To do this he took thousands of pictures of hogs at ten- to twenty-minute intervals. He determined if a hog hasn't moved during that time, it's "comfortable."

(As opposed to dead, which also generally restricts a hog's movement.)

Xin fed his data into a computer that analyzed these porky glamour shots and told him something amazing: The hogs themselves let you know when they're happy. You just have to read their body language.

Xin's research verified what common sense has told us for years: When pigs are too hot they increase the space between them. When they're too cold they huddle together for warmth.

Quick! Call Mr. Wizard! Get NASA on the phone! Reserve the Nobel Prize!

Now mankind can tell how comfortable hogs are by how close together they hang out.

Pig producers are jumping for joy. Feedlots across the pork-consuming world are abuzz with the news. Farmer Brown won't have to guess anymore if his porkers are pleased. He can just take a peek in the pen and say, "Turn up the heat, Helen, the hogs is huddling again."

According to a spokesman for the Iowa Pork Producers, Xin's work is a breakthrough because it "will allow us to fine-tune the system and ask the pig what is most comfortable."

Ask the pigs what would make them comfortable?

I'm no scientist myself, but I'm guessing if you took a hog survey, they'd probably say all that temperature control business is fine, but lifting that built-in death sentence would really put a smile on their faces.

Home, Sweet Home

My son just bought a house. I thought I'd write him a note.

Dear Hunter,

Congratulations! Buying a home is the biggest investment you'll ever make, not to mention a giant leap into the adult world of maturity, responsibility and…insanity.

Home ownership is called "The American Dream" with good reason. But at times it can seem like The American Nightmare. As one who has experienced the dark side of home ownership, I thought I'd pass along a few tips that weren't included in the thousands of papers you signed when you closed your loan.

Remember, Rome wasn't built in a day. Neither was your home. But sometimes it will seem like it's falling apart overnight. Houses are like people. As they get older, they creak, groan, warp, bend and begin to lose parts. Unlike people, houses can be put back together by anyone with a high tolerance for pain, frustration and heartache.

Expect problems to surface at the worst possible times. For instance, sooner or later, your home's air-conditioning system will—without warning—wheeze, gurgle, gasp and give up the ghost. This will always happen on the hottest day in the last 20 years. Guaranteed.

A well-prepared homeowner can postpone repairs until winter, when rates are much lower. During hot months, just keep the house stocked with lots of water and ice.

Speaking of ice, you can probably collect plenty during the largest ice storm of the last 20 years, which is when your furnace will fail.

But not all home disasters are major. You will have small repairs that can be corrected with a few basic tools, beginning with a paintbrush.

Your house has lovely wood siding and trim. Sooner or later, it will need maintenance. This means painting. Plan ahead. Visit several home improvement stores right now and choose your favorite brand of paint.

Then buy stock in the paint company. Over the years, this will beat your 401(k) hands down.

For other maintenance needs, you will need a few basic tools. I suggest a hammer, a saw, a screwdriver, a drill and a blender.

For many reasons—including gravity—things fall off houses. Shutters, ceiling fans, cupboard doors, towel bars, people, etcetera. Except for the people, you can use your hammer to put them back up. You can use your saw to cut the low-lying tree limbs the squirrels use to enter your attic and eat your wiring and short out the electricity and set your house on fire.

The drill is handy for making holes to hang up new things to replace the old things that fall off. The screwdriver can tighten or loosen some of the millions of screws in the house that will become tighter or looser with age. It is also good for taking a door off its hinges, which sooner or later, will have to be done. (Have I told you the story about when your sister was a baby and got trapped in her room?)

You will use many (if not all) of your tools in the bathroom, for reasons you can't yet fathom and I won't include here.

Your yard is small. Mowers are expensive and tend to break. Consider a goat.

Finally, termites can literally destroy your house. Destroy them first, using whatever tool feels right. Then use your hammer and saw to put the house back together again.

I almost forgot the blender. Use this as needed after especially brutal repair jobs to make frozen rum drinks with umbrellas in them. Then, sit in the yard and sip your drink and remember the good old days. When you were a renter.

Finally, and I can't stress this enough, at all times, you should have plenty, and I mean plenty, of duct tape. That stuff will patch anything but a broken heart.

If you have problems, don't hesitate to let me know. I'll help you all I can. Over the phone.

Love, Dad

Flushed with Fear

The stories must have started the day after the first one was installed. Everyone has a toilet tale. Not a potty-mouthed joke but a true-life saga involving the eternal struggle between man and everyone's favorite modern convenience.

Mine mostly involve unwelcome overflows at inopportune times, but the one about the book isn't bad. I'd just moved into a brand new apartment and the toilet started backing up immediately. The maintenance man had to remove the entire appliance to find the problem, which turned out to be a pornographic paperback novel allegedly left behind by construction workers.

One of my favorite tales involves a former neighbor. The way she tells it, her life had been free of toilet trauma until that fateful day when...

She was in the tub and heard a noise coming from the general direction of the john. She arose to check it out and when she looked down, instead of a peaceful puddle, found herself staring straight at...well, something.

From her description it was either an overweight rat or an anorexic possum. But whatever it was, it was soaking wet and gasping for air and doing its best to jump out of the john and into her stylishly decorated bathroom suite. Since her daily schedule didn't include battling an unruly rodent, she slammed the lid, screamed loudly and proceeded to call the National Guard, the *National Enquirer*, a plumber, and the Georgia Department of Fish and Game.

The creature was finally dispatched, but to this day my friend still trembles as she approaches the toilet. Can't blame her.

Critters in the john are more common than you might think. Everyone knows New Yorkers have a fondness for flushing baby gators down the drain, and each year you hear that a few manage to find their way back to their former homes. (The rest turn into 100-foot-long monsters that share the city's sewer system with local politicians.)

I saw a Discovery Channel special not long ago that documented cases of poisonous snakes crawling out of Australian toilets and fishes swimming upstream to roost in Russian appliances.

But while possums, rats or snakes are bad, it has come to my attention that a certain toilet in Asia is home to something even more horrifying. At least to me. For my money, it doesn't get much worse than finding out Satan is camped out in your commode.

According to the Reuters News Agency, it's happened in the village of Kapurawala, India. The story says terrified parents have pulled their daughters out of the local government girls' school after becoming convinced the toilet was home to the Prince of Darkness.

Suspicions first arose after three girls suffered epileptic fits shortly after using the toilet. A teacher left the school as well, saying she was "gripped by fear" that an evil spirit prowled the plumbing.

Sub-Inspector of Police Hakim Singh told United News of India: "Nobody has seen the ghost, but the school toilet, suspected to be the devil's den, was brought down by villagers."

What he meant was, the villagers didn't call for a government study or appeal for a federal toilet grant. They simply tore the toilet out of the floor, then took it outside and pounded it into porcelain pebbles.

But they're still not satisfied. Some of the elders think the spirit of Satan still haunts the entire school. They say the only way to drive out the spirit for good is to perform a "Yagya," or fire purification ceremony.

Which means they intend to build a huge bonfire inside the school to drive out any remaining demons. That ought to do it, but let's hope things don't get out of control. In fact, it might be best if they just stood in the bathroom and flicked their Bics.

Satan in the toilet is bad, but a school in ashes might be worse.

The Big Question is Finally Answered

Whales have been big news ever since Jonah used one as a bed-and-breakfast. And not just big news but big business. Throughout recorded history, men have found the seagoing monsters useful for everything from feeding Eskimos to furnishing some sort of greasy substance highly prized by perfume vendors.

That popularity had a downside, however, and by the early part of the twentieth century, certain species of whale had been hunted almost to extinction. Luckily for whales, their looming demise occurred at the birth of the environmental movement.

According to my sources, the first modern-day whale lover was Mary Kay Barfbucket, of Sandhill, South Dakota, who, in 1966, discovered marijuana, changed her name to Sister Serendipity and moved to San Francisco, where she discovered peace, love and LSD.

She was quoted in a now extinct hippie newspaper as saying she really dug whales because they were "really big" and looked "really awesome. Especially if you had some good acid, dude."

Before you know it, the "Save the Whales" movement was born, complete with membership cards, T-shirts and secret handshake.

There was just one problem. Whales could swim and splash and took up lots of space but they didn't do tricks and didn't bark like seals or even groan like mating elephants. On the public relations circuit, whales were a disaster because they were silent. Or so the world thought.

Then came a breakthrough discovery. Whales didn't talk, they did something better. They sang.

They weren't exactly seagoing Sinatras, but they beat heavy metal hands down. Recordings were made of their bellows, bleats and coos and one disc, *Songs of the Humpback Whale*, actually cracked the top ten on the Billboard list of Irrelevant New Age Songs. But once the singing started, questions followed. The main one being, "What are they saying?"

Scientists figured the whales were trying to communicate, but since whales weren't known to discuss politics, religion or even sports, the test tube jockeys had no idea what all the chatting was about.

Until now. The riddle is solved. At least to my satisfaction.

Thanks go to Andrew Bass, a Cornell University neurobiologist, who doesn't fool with whales but has spent years studying the toadfish, which lives in the Pacific Ocean from California to Alaska.

In addition to being spectacularly ugly, the toadfish is also renowned for making a humming sound by vibrating a set of muscles on its air bladders. The toadfish can do this six thousand times a minute. For up to an hour at a time.

After years of study, Bass finally figured the toadfish wasn't just whistling "Dixie." It was sending the world's oldest message, the undersea equivalent of "Hey, baby, what's your sign? Your place or mine?" Yep, the so-called "song" of the toadfish is nothing but a cheap attempt to get a date.

It seems logical the whales are wailing for the same reason. Kind of like teenage boys who roll through town with music blaring at deafening levels out of car speakers the size of refrigerators.

This breakthrough in interspecies understanding should be good news, but I wonder?

What will people think once they learn whales are no more artistically inspired than a fire hydrant? Could be damaging to their image.

On the bright side, though, people who live near toadfish populations would like to see them and their obnoxious noises nuked out of existence. Whales emit pleasant sounds.

At least for now.

Right now they may be the Barry Whites of the wet set, but what if whales discover hip-hop? Imagine a 100-ton Snoop Doggy Dogg showing up at your favorite stretch of beach.

Whale watching might be more popular than ever, but I have a feeling that instead of binoculars and cameras, the crowd might be carrying harpoons.

Household Horrors Explained?

If you live long enough, almost every question you ever had will eventually be answered.

This particular mystery goes all the way back to my college days and involved a refrigerator that, at times, produced more than cold air. The appliance lived with three guys who lived in an old house across the alley from the old house my roommates and I shared. They said the icebox never actually burst into flames but had a nasty tendency to spark, snort, sizzle and smoke without the least provocation.

One of my roommates thought it was a matter of old age. At the time, it sounded feasible since the refrigerator was so old its serial number was in Roman numerals. Another roommate, who said he was experienced in electrical matters and had personally used jumper cables to power an ice cream churn, said the fault wasn't with the appliance but the home's ancient wiring.

He insisted "power surges" were overloading the machine's circuits, causing the confusion and combustion that threatened to burn our buddies to death about once a week.

In a rare moment of self-preservation, the guys finally bought an extra long extension cord and moved the refrigerator to the yard. That's where it was when it finally burned itself to a crisp. I wasn't there, but I hear the guys salvaged their supply of cold beer, called some friends and held a pep rally, complete with bonfire.

I hadn't thought about it since. Until now.

And now, I'm convinced those refrigerator problems ran deeper than originally thought.

In fact, they may have run all the way back to the priest. Or at least he's an Episcopal priest now. Back then, he was a religion student. And somewhat of a dabbler.

"Bob" (not his real name) loved to scare us with tales of demons, witches, spirits and other things he eventually went on to do professional battle with.

One night, he asked if he could try and summon evil spirits into our crib. Since none of us had the least interest in spending quality time with Satan or any of his posse, we passed. He went across the alley and the other guys said, "Why not?"

After the "ceremony" was over, we checked things out. "Bob" was drinking a beer and Satan wasn't sitting in the chair, so we figured the ritual was a flop. But was it?

Recent news reports from Sicily seem to indicate that where Satan is concerned, appliances may be Home Sweet Home on earth. In fact, things have gotten so bad in the Sicilian village of Canneto that the entire town has been evacuated following a string of mysterious fires that broke out over a span of three weeks. Fires blazed in everything from televisions to washing machines to yes...even refrigerators.

When the suspicious fires began, village officials looked for scientific explanations. And came up dead empty. The town's civil protection chief, Tullio Matrella, was quoted in the *Scotsman* newspaper as saying, "There is no scientific explanation for it, and I have never heard of anything like this happening before."

After doing everything from testing individual home electrical circuits to shutting down the town's electric railway system, the population threw up their hands and declared there was only one explanation: The devil did it.

Then they hired an exorcist with experience in possessed appliances.

Gabriele Amorth is an official Catholic exorcist who claims to have seen the phenomenon before. When interviewed about the mysterious fires, he said, "With cases of demon behavior, it is normal for domestic appliances to be involved. Let's not forget, that Satan and his followers have immense powers."

Wow. I always heard the devil was in the details, but in the dishwasher? Now that's a scary notion.

Dangerous Dining

Science fiction movies have changed a lot since I was a kid. Nowadays, big-screen monsters ooze all kinds of rancid goo from their pores and have heads inside of heads and bore into people's guts and could probably kill most normal humans by just grossing them out.

Years ago, it was a kinder, gentler alien world, filled with green-skinned, bug-eyed perpetrators who mostly wanted to take over the earth and ravish its women. When they needed to waste a human, they used a tried-and-true technique...death rays fired from buzzing, pulsing cosmic six-shooters. I think some of the rays even came out the aliens' eyeballs. I can't remember.

I do remember it taught me a lasting lesson: That invisible rays can be harmful to your health.

Which is why I'm disturbed over the latest food fad.

It's called irradiation, and basically it does to food what aliens used to do to humans...it zaps it. This kills the bacteria that live on food. People say this procedure is needed. Like the folks who died after ingesting E. coli-tainted beef in the Midwest. Or the group of worshippers who dropped like flies at a salmonella-soaked church supper.

Government officials have heard the pleas. They have vowed to save us. Even if it means blasting our food with nuclear death rays.

I protest. I am against glow-in-the-dark food. I don't care for my tenderloin to double as a refrigerator light. Sure, a handful of folks croak every year from bad eats, but that's life.

If the government is serious about saving lives, they should invent a portable death ray that citizens could carry around to sterilize such truly harmful things as public toilets and opera singers, both of which pose a bigger threat to America than the occasional bad burger.

I'm against this high-tech hocus-pocus. Partly because it's unnatural, and partly because ever since my vasectomy, I get squeamish at the mention of sterilization.

That said, I have to admit that in light of a recent happening, the thought of making food safer, by whatever means, has been a little more appealing.

The problem began when my employment contract required that I put my cooking skills on public display. I did so by assaulting a sweet potato. I heated it up, then mashed it, then sampled my work.

It tasted fine at the time, but hours later I was racked with chills, fever and some generally unpleasant digestive turmoil. Since I hadn't consumed anything else, I figured my symptoms were spud-related.

But the potato came from a clean, modern supermarket. It looked nice and healthy. How could it have been bad?

Aha, I thought. Perhaps the problem wasn't with the potato but the preparation. A real possibility in light of my rather unusual kitchen technique. You see, instead of resorting to conventional methods, I mashed my potato by placing a 2 x 6 on top of it and pounding the lumber with a hammer until the vegetable was rendered flat and harmless. After careful consideration, I believe the fact that the hammer was rusty and the 2 x 6 was covered with grease and gray paint may have caused some contamination problems and my subsequent discomfort.

I now believe this could have been avoided had my potato—not to mention the hammer and the board—been subjected to a dose of the death ray.

Looking back on that night, I wish my food had been irradiated. Or consecrated or mutilated or anything else to make it safe. Because that one bad sweet potato had me really hurting, and as I lay there, bowels groaning and belly churning, I longed for only one thing.

The silence of the yams.

BUSINESS: RISKY, BAD, RUTHLESS AND RIDICULOUS

In addition to business as usual, this section mentions lawyers,
and the business of law. Some of my friends are lawyers.
I love them anyway.

Bad Eyes are Bad News for Men's Mag

I was ten and miserable and as I walked out of the optometrist's office, sporting my first set of spectacles, the first thing I saw was my mother's face. I knew the faint smile was her way of saying, "I told you so."

A few years earlier, in another town, Danny Sander was my best friend, and we were inseparable. When we weren't riding bikes or building forts or trapping crayfish, we loved to sneak into his parents' bedroom and rustle through the closet where Danny's father stored his supply of *Esquire* magazines.

Sometimes we spent hours gazing bug-eyed at pictures of scantily clad or sometimes buck-naked women. The photos in those vintage *Esquires* would seem positively puritanical by today's gynecologically explicit standards, but in the pre-*Playboy* era, they were as hot as it got.

One day Mother and I dropped by together, and while she and Danny's mom chatted about PTA, he and I headed straight for the bedroom closet. We were deep in the throes of pictorial lust when Mother burst in unexpectedly...and promptly hit the roof.

I knew what was coming, but after the boilerplate hellfire and damnation lecture, she added a new wrinkle that got my attention. "If you keep doing that," she said in menacing tones, "you'll go blind."

It was years before I realized she wasn't talking about eyestrain from squinting at the fine print. And even after countless science classes, I always wondered if my myopia wasn't due, at least in part, to ogling those *Esquires.*

Now I've decided it doesn't matter. All that matters is that my eyes are bad. And that it may finally be possible—due to new trends in litigation— to collect a bundle for a lifetime of pain, suffering and blurred vision. And who better to reimburse me than the party which harmed me, namely *Esquire* magazine and its parent company, the Hearst Corporation, whose pockets are damn near as deep as Bill Gates's.

Those smut slingers at Hearst Publishing knew exactly what was happening to my eyes as I gazed at each piece of gauzy negligee and strained over each fold of flesh. Any juror with half a brain could see I've got a huge case worthy of a huge settlement. All I need is the right lawyer. I think I know just the man.

Mr. Samuel Hirsch, of New York, should be available as soon as he finishes representing fellow New Yorker Caesar Barber in a similar case of gross consumer negligence. The 272-pound Barber claims his two heart attacks and diabetes are the result of a conspiracy by the fast-food industry. With Hirsch's assistance, he is suing Wendy's, McDonald's, Burger King and Kentucky Fried Chicken for breach of health.

Barber claims he had no idea a grease-soaked chicken wing or fat-dripping burger wasn't as healthy as raw broccoli sprouts. "They said '100 percent beef.' I thought that meant it was good for you," Barber told *Newsday*. He told the *New York Times*, "The fast-food industry has wrecked my life."

Attorney Hirsch nutshelled his case by saying, "There is direct deception when someone omits telling people food digested is detrimental to their health." Since Hirsch was my potential lawyer, I was pleased to see he cleverly ignored the fact that since the Nutrition Labeling and Education Act was passed 12 years ago, the restaurants named in the suit have provided nutritional labeling for all their products, including the salads and low-fat foods that Barber is obviously opposed to ingesting.

Some say this type of legal action is hard to swallow. But they don't understand. This is America. And I am damaged. Which means somebody, somewhere, owes me. All I can say is, open your wallet, *Esquire*. And make it a supersized check. I don't want to have to squint to read all the zeros.

Shopping Spree

The Stone Age I understood. You took a rock and either made a tool from it or killed your neighbor with it. Pretty simple stuff.

I even halfway understood the Age of Aquarius. It had something to do with long hair and drugs. It's our current age I'm having trouble with.

You know...the Information Age. I'm sick of it. Beaming promoters say that a world of information is just a mouse twitch away. That it's way cool that I can now dial up the Internet and find out the temperature in some sheep ranch in China. Big deal.

Give me something useful, like how long until the check clears or why do women drive that way. All this other so-called "information," I don't need.

I can find worthless facts all day long. What I can't find is somebody to add two and two. At least I couldn't the other day.

I went to a large chain store to make a small purchase. When I couldn't find what I wanted, I asked for "information" and was told where to search. After three more stops for "information," I grabbed the gadget and headed out.

I found a checkout stand with no waiting and plopped my purchase down. The friendly, informative clerk smiled, turned the box over to expose the little zebra-like bar code, whipped out her infrared ray gun and zapped my package. No response. She zapped again. The machine buzzed and grunted, but nothing came up on her computer screen.

Her attempts to enter the number by hand resulted in an electronic belch. Frantic, she punched in every number printed on the box, and many that weren't, including the secret nuclear codes for the destruction of New Jersey. I think it was her Fantasy Five number from the night before that finally caused the machine to jingle and chime and spit out a number.

"That'll be $209.96." She smiled triumphantly.

"For this piece of rubber hose?" I said. "I don't think so." I told her the price on the shelf was $19.96, trying to be helpful, giving her some "information."

She explained the machine didn't understand prices, only stock numbers, and was helpless without them.

By now the line behind me was piling up with surly people, glaring at

me because I dared try to check out with damaged "information." A spare
employee was dispatched to find a duplicate item with a readable bar code.
In five minutes the runner returned, breathless and empty-handed. She
asked me to show her where I'd found my prize. We left to the cheers of
customers waiting in line with good information.

I found the aisle. I found the box. My helper looked at it.

"This one looks good," she said.

"The hose?" I asked.

"No, the bar code. Let's go."

We returned and handed the box to a customer service rep, who
whipped her wand over my item. Nothing. And again and again. Even
when assured the item cost $19.96, she was stuck, said her machine needed
more "information."

Finally, after an extended bout of electronic punch-out, the machine
spat forth a number close to the actual purchase price. The clerk beamed.
I heaved. I got my piece of hose. The store got my money. And their "information."

I've had it with this computerized con game.

This Information Age business has gone far enough. When you can't
even make a simple purchase because the computers don't get the right information, something's haywire. I say it's time to go back to the real world.
Back to less "information" and more common sense.

Give me some guy who makes change out of a cigar box. Somebody
who won't ask for my information, just my money. That's all I need, or
want, information-wise.

And as for that big chain store that gave me so much trouble...here's a
piece of "information" for them: I won't be back.

Dangerous Drawers

Mr. Calvin Klein
General Delivery
New York City

Dear Calvin,

Normally I hate to impose on high-profile types like yourself. Being a media celebrity myself, I know what it's like to contend with hordes of egg-throwing fans at lunch. But at this point, your privacy is no longer my concern. I've got a problem, and it needs your attention.

I'm about to leave town on a critical journalistic-type assignment. That's the good part. Here's the bad: When I began packing, I did something I rarely do. I actually looked at my underwear.

Normally, it just sits around in a couple of piles...clean on the couch, dirty on the floor. And when the floor pile is big enough, I wash a few sets of drawers and dump them on the couch. I run through them all without looking at them. Frankly, I don't care what they look like.

But like I said, I'm doing this trip. And where I'm heading, one never knows when a motel chambermaid or pervert type might get the urge to scrutinize one's drawers. So I wanted to make sure I took the good ones.

And there's my problem in a nutshell. The good ones. I don't seem to have any. At least none I deem travel-worthy. I'm sure you know the rule about wearing clean drawers in case you have a wreck. Well, mine, even after a dose of Cheer, look like they've already been in a wreck.

So I bit the bullet, admitted my drawers were in disrepair and set out to correct the problem. Mostly by buying some new ones. Big mistake. Obviously, it's been a while since I patronized the underwear section of a store.

Last time I looked there were two choices...boxers or briefs.

Calvin, those days are history, and it looks to me like you've led the charge in underwear evolution. That's why I'm writing you.

First, what's the deal with all these new styles? It looks as if some fashion design team from hell has been working overtime to come up with nifty duds for a part of the body that used to go mostly unseen. What's up with that? A man used to get by with a couple of leg holes and a waist. No more.

Why all the different styles? And who's supposed to notice? Are people showing these things off nowadays?

And how's a person to know what style is right for them? When boxers and briefs were the only choice it was simple. Briefs for the left-lobed accountant types and boxers for the free spirits, the artsy types, the swingers.

But now, there are mid-length, over-the-calf, under-the-armpit, around-the-horn and God knows what else. There are brief boxers and boxer briefs and some jobs that are so tight you'd have to grease yourself just to get them on.

There are even bikini panties for dudes. You've seen those slingshot looking things European sissies wear to the beach? These are the same, except you wear them around the house or the office.

I don't know where to turn. And if the styles weren't enough, I also have to make another choice...color. What ever happened to white? OK, I can understand why old guys like me prefer the earthier tones, but why so many?

Why have you done this, Cal? Is it to attract chicks? Or, in your case, guys? Come on, man. I was raised to believe some things should be neither seen nor heard, underwear included.

I've got to deal with news, sports and weather, Calvin. I don't need this. I hope you'll send me an e-mail or something and explain which style is best for a tired old unromantic geek.

And I know you're busy, but please answer quickly. The tangerine-colored French cuts at Kmart are beginning to grow on me.

Yours For Glamorous Groins,
Alex McRae

Here Come the Judge

When she was happy, my mother's smile could melt glaciers. But when she was angry, her heart could chip diamonds. Gray wasn't her shade. She saw things in black and white and didn't suffer fools gladly. She would have loved these two news items...

In the first, one eight-year-old Little Leaguer is suing another for an accidental bang with a baseball bat. In the second, the parents of a 16-year-old girl are suing the mother of the boy who got the girl pregnant, seeking to recover medical expenses, including the cost of the abortion.

Twenty years ago, the Little League incident would have been settled with an apology and an ice bag, the pregnancy problem with a shotgun wedding. But it's the nineties, and nowadays, we solve our problems with lawsuits.

I have a couple of ideas why. First, because a glut of lawyers has left us with a group of client-starved, fee-hungry legal parasites who constantly troll for victims, advertising their wares on late-night TV and billboards blaring such catchy legalisms as "Had A Wreck? Get A Check."

The second reason Americans are suit-happy is because juries have too often awarded huge sums in even the most frivolous cases, leaving people with the impression that the legal pot of gold is within everyone's reach.

Bored lawyers and bad juries. I have a feeling we'd have fewer of both if my mother had something to say about it. She did once. It was over twenty years ago, and by that time, severe rheumatoid arthritis and osteoporosis had left her body shrunken and withered, but her mind was clear as spring water and she never hesitated to use it.

Soon after my father died she moved to Savannah to live with her sister. Her first two acts in her new hometown were to join the Baptist church across the street and register to vote. The latter act landed her squarely in the Chatham County jury pool. When she was called on to render her civic duty, she did it with relish.

The case she heard involved a husband, a wife and a car wreck. The accident had ruined a car and put the woman in the hospital for a few days. It was pretty much cut and dried, and the traffic end of the case had been settled to everyone's satisfaction.

Except, it seems, for the husband, who viewed his wife's motoring escapade as not just a mangling of sheet metal but an opportunity to retire early on someone else's dime. On the advice of legal counsel, he brought suit for something called "loss of consort," which, in layman's terms, meant the mental anguish caused by the wreck had left the wife either unable or unwilling to perform her romantic duties. The husband decided that cash was the only thing that could sustain him during his sexual fast.

Mother said the husband was crabby and the wife was worse, a neck-braced nightmare filled with bile who moaned constantly during the proceedings, wincing and whining as she sought sympathy from the assembled jurors.

She found not a shred in Erie McRae. Mother said when the jury retired she told the other members of the panel if they ever intended to see their families again, they'd better belch out a "not guilty" verdict, because she certainly wasn't going to change her mind.

They did, and the man seeking damages for loss of consort was left to seek relief elsewhere than the courtroom.

Mother summed up her judicial argument nicely, saying, "That woman was so crabby, I don't know why anybody would want to consort with her, anyway."

Aah. Common sense. Too bad we don't see a little more of it these days.

As Wrong as It Gets

When I was in college, he showed up about every other Sunday, a little man with a three-day growth of beard, a homemade haircut, and a sign around his neck that said, "Repent. The End Is Near."

That was years ago but the message is still around. Every day we're deluged with brimstone-spouting preachers, TV specials about Nostradamus, and tabloid horror stories, all of them claiming extinction is imminent.

Now the millennium boosters have put the gloom-and-doom machinery in high gear, saying that come the year 2000, the human race is gonna cash in its chips and close down the old global casino. I can't buy it. I'd be worried if God had personally done our calendar, but I think it was worked up by a bunch of old dead dudes who might have skipped a few years, so I'm sure there's room for error.

But still, I watch for other signs. And I've noticed some minor stuff, like the fact that the US military is now more concerned with sensitivity than sharpshooting, and people are reading books like *Bridges of Madison County*. Bad news, but not earthshaking.

I was waiting for the really big stuff, like birds flying north instead of south for the winter, the media declaring Elvis permanently dead, or something even more bizarre, like a politician passing a polygraph test.

Turns out I was looking in the wrong place. The most fearsome sign that the end is near was right under my nose.

It was Sunday night. I'd been working late, and around the stroke of midnight I decided some chow was in order and lugged myself out to a place where the food's quick and good and the waitresses are generally glad to see you.

I ordered two eggs over medium, bacon and hash browns. About halfway through my order of scattered and smothered, I heard it...the sound of doom.

At first I thought it was coming from the parking lot, a diesel, maybe, with a fouled glowplug. In time it became obvious the problem wasn't outside but in, emanating from the bowels of the jukebox.

Louder and louder it pulsed, nagging and rancid, like a recording of Satan trying to hack up a phlegm ball. I listened in horror until it dawned on me that the world had indeed gone mad. No other explanation for...

Rap music at the Waffle House.

Hand on the Bible. At the Waffle House, where opening day means deer, not baseball, where over easy is an order of eggs and not a description of Bill Clinton's female companions, where they always say "Good morning," even when it's not, where the grease and smoke are always thick in the air.

This stuff wasn't music but more like a recording of a distressed colon, gurgling over and over something that sounded like "Yo" and "In the hoooouuuse."

I was crushed. My whole life, Waffle House music was Hank and George and Merle and maybe Engelbert or the Four Tops or Smokey. Real music by people with real names, not nasal, whiny, monotonous, hiccup-sounding noises by people with handles like U2 Fine, EZ Open, T-Ice or Biggie Phat.

Most restaurants have installed No Smoking sections as a sop to the health nuts. I call on Waffle House to declare a No Rap policy on the same basis. After all, there is scientific proof that rap is more harmful to one's health than cholesterol ever was. Don't believe me? Check the obits under "Slain Gangsta."

Until the WH does an about-face I guess I'll have to settle for Rooty Tooty Fresh and Fruity. Not a manly sounding meal, but filling all the same. Either that or just shut up, do like Mother said, and be thankful for the small things.

Here's one. At least my bill wasn't $6.66.

Look for Naked Next

Maybe not this week and maybe not this year, but sooner or later, the business suit will give way to the birthday suit. We're halfway there already.

The American workplace is undergoing a fashion revolution. The gray flannel three-piece and four-inch heels are becoming endangered faster than the spotted owl. Employee manuals dictating shirt colors and skirt lengths are about as politically correct as a Klan rally.

It's a reflection of the times. Modern workers refuse to feel cramped by ancient stereotypes. They want to display their individuality, their uniqueness, their sense of self. And beyond body piercing or tattooing, nothing says "This is me" like a set of duds.

And so employers seeking to keep their company cubicles crammed with happy faces instituted the custom known as "casual Friday."

To be honest, I originally applauded the idea. I've never felt that a person's performance was connected to their choice of designer labels.

I could even cite health reasons for going casual. It's common knowledge that neckties are like mental tourniquets and can lead to constipation of the brain, gas and in severe cases, mental disorders of postal magnitude. Ditto pantyhose, which my female acquaintances tell me are not just tight and hot and annoying but the leading cause of domestic violence and PMS.

I saw no harm in banishing the Brooks Brothers or Donna Karans to the closet once a week for a clothing sabbath. But perhaps the pendulum has swung a few yards too far. Casual Friday is rapidly becoming casual every day. At some businesses, the office portrait looks like it could have been taken at a reunion for the local homeless shelter.

There are exceptions, but as a general rule, this is not good for consumer confidence. If your workday is spent under the grease rack or behind the meat counter slaughtering sheep, casual is fine, even necessary. But there are certain professions where a minimum of dress decorum is called for.

For instance, I would hate for the attorney arguing my whiplash claim to confront a jury of my peers while wearing a tie-dyed T-shirt and a pair of cut-off Levis. The thought of a corporate titan committing a hostile takeover while dressed in a set of Speedos leaves me cold. And I don't even want to think about my banker making loans in a loincloth.

And what if this trend sweeps the funeral home industry? Who, in their hour of grief, wants to be consoled by a perky pitchman hawking perpetual care while clad in a gaudy Hawaiian shirt and a baseball cap with "Don't Worry, Be Happy" embroidered across the bill.

For my money this round of workplace strip poker has gone far enough. But I realize that once the casual cat is out of the bag, it's hard to put it back.

And if that's the case, and if this trend lurches to its logical conclusion, don't be surprised if office conversations like this become commonplace:

"Ms. Snarfle, take a letter."

"Yes, Mr. Smith, right away. OK, boss, I'm ready."

"Hmmm."

"I said I'm ready. Excuse me, Mr. Smith, but are you OK? Why are you staring at me?"

"Ms. Snarfle, you're not wearing a brassiere."

"I beg your pardon?"

"I couldn't help but notice you're not wearing a brassiere."

"Of course not, you chauvinist, sexist pig. Haven't you heard? It's the nineties. We women are free to express ourselves any way we want. Besides, where have you been? I haven't worn a bra all year."

"I know, but before today, at least you've worn a blouse."

Clothes don't make the man (or the woman), but where business is concerned, surely bare bottoms won't help the bottom line.

DINING AND ART, FINE AND OTHERWISE

If you've eaten something other than fast food and your interest in "art" extends beyond paint by numbers, you'll understand these stories. Except for the ones about art.

A Sad Seafood Saga

The snowdrifts were thick and skiers had finished their last runs of the day. Parties of two, four and five gathered to celebrate day's end with cold beer and hot buttered rum. Christmas was approaching, and patrons of the Chowda House in Littleton, Colorado, were in a festive mood as they anticipated the evening's main event: a raffle to save a life.

Or at least a lobster.

The object of this humanitarian effort was Bob, a Maine native who had somehow found his way to the lobster tank of the Chowda House. At ten pounds, Bob was considered a little too old and tough for most diners' tastes, and after a couple of months, he became something of a celebrity. Well-intentioned locals decided to raise some money for charity and churn up a little goodwill by raffling off Bob, with the agreement that he would be set free back in his old New England home.

A United Airlines pilot with an obvious crush on the critter volunteered to airlift Bob to Boston, where he would be released with a hail of publicity and warm, fuzzy feelings.

Obviously the pilot did not offer the lobster luxury accommodations. I say this because at the end of the flight, Bob was missing one of his parts, namely a claw, which somehow became dislodged during the flight. Experts say it may have been shucked as a defense mechanism against excessive handling.

Once the plane landed, things got worse. That's when Bob's buddies took him for a short boat ride. Then, before a sea of cameras, with great fanfare and humanity, they hoisted the crippled crustacean in triumph before dropping him into the murky depths of Boston Harbor.

Viewers watching on live TV were appalled to see that not only was Bob an accidental amputee, but his remaining claw was still wrapped in those rubber band things that people put on live lobsters to keep them from destroying small children and pets before they (the lobsters) are boiled to death.

The outrage was quick and vicious. Viewers began calling in to both WHDH in Boston and KUSA in Denver, voicing their concerns over the way Bob had been treated, furious that the lobster was not only dismembered, but defenseless.

It was a disaster. Stung by the bad publicity, the Colorado crusaders brought forth a lobster biologist from the New England Aquarium to plead their case. The expert, Mr. Jason Goldstein, said that eventually the rubber band would work its way off Bob's remaining claw, and until then, Bob could use his legs to zip around in search of food.

Biologist Goldstein said of the attempted rescue, "It was a good gesture, but they didn't do their homework. Obviously, it would have been better to release a healthy lobster with two claws and no rubber band."

Chowda House co-owner David Francavilla, who accompanied Bob on his emancipation tour, was distressed that his intended good deed had caused ill will. "We thought it was a real noble cause," he said. "To raise money for charity and release the lobster to live out his last few decades."

Unfortunately, decades may not be in Bob's future. In a final foul-up, Bob was deposited in a patch of ocean populated not only by other lobsters but by thousands of commercial lobster traps.

Chances are, he'll be caught again. His only hope is that discerning lobstermen will throw him back, realizing a one-legged lobster doesn't fetch top dollar at the dining table.

I'm certain there were good intentions all around, but looking back, it might have been better if Bob had just been boiled back home.

Art is Where You Find It

New York was just what I needed. During a recent not-long-enough weekend in Manhattan I managed to catch up with some old friends, sample some fabulous food, listen to some great music and walk my legs off, including a late-afternoon spin through Central Park in the snow.

I gave my eyeballs a treat as well by exposing them to some visual art. The Metropolitan Museum was only a couple of blocks from where I stayed, and I made three visits. The traveling exhibits that stop in Atlanta are nice, but viewing some of the world's greatest art treasures in their permanent lodgings was a totally different experience.

In the Met, the great paintings and sculptures seemed relaxed and comfortable in their peaceful surroundings. Even the transplanted Egyptian temple felt right at home in uptown Manhattan.

The Old Masters exceeded my expectations. Ditto the more "modern" offerings, which were even worse than I expected. Andy Warhol's high-priced Xeroxes were as cheesy and insipid in person as they appear in print, and Jackson Pollock's splatterings, which shook the art world in the mid twentieth century, looked like used drop cloths from a house-painting project. Just bigger.

I decided to dabble in some cutting edge stuff but only made it as far as a collection of nude photos. They were considered trendy because the photographer posed his models in positions that would have taxed a yoga master and shot them in sections from quirky angles, creating an effect that left you wondering if you were looking at a human being or an arrangement of overripe, flesh-covered fruit.

I didn't make it to the truly avant-garde offerings at the Met, but I guess it wouldn't have mattered. I've just learned that while I was in New York gaping at Gauguin, one of the art world's hottest commodities was half a country away.

The artist in question is Mr. Adam Zaretsky, of San Francisco, whose one-man exhibition recently played to large crowds in Salina, Kansas. Of course it's hard to tell whether the crowds were there to see Zaretsky or an armadillo, perhaps a prairie dog.

His exhibit was staged in the middle of the local zoo. Titled "The Workhorse Zoo," Zaretsky's offering consists of an eight-by-eight-foot glass cube inhabited by several families of mice, a few albino frogs and a yeast culture. The prime tenant is Mr. Zaretsky, starring in his role as "Zed, species homo sapiens."

While the mice chased their tails and the albino frogs blinked and hopped and the yeast did whatever yeast does, Zaretsky wowed the crowd for a week by reclining on a hospital gurney and watching his guests watch him.

Zaretsky explained that his exhibit is an attempt to "blur the boundary between what is human culture and what is reality." He says he hopes the display will "get people thinking about their relationships with other living things."

Certainly got me thinking along those lines. And I've decided if Zaretsky is ever in my neighborhood, our relationship will be that of unwelcome guest (him) and the person who avoids him studiously (me).

And it could be the people who stopped to stare weren't there to watch Zaretsky but his assistant, Julia Reodica, who acted as the exhibit's "zookeeper." Clad in a Boy Scout uniform and long, black zip-up boots, Reodica stood in front of the exhibit, warning viewers about its temperamental star, saying that when agitated, Zaretsky "throws rubbish against the windows."

Glad it's only rubbish. Last time I visited the zoo, the monkeys were throwing things at viewers, too, but it wasn't garbage. Of course you've gotta give the monkeys credit...at least they didn't try to pass it off as art.

Food for Thought

The last time I was in New York some friends raved about a new deli sandwich. I checked it out. It was a monster, a half pound of deli meat between slices of dark rye, splashed with lettuce and tomato and slathered with a "secret" mixture of condiments.

It looked great. But I couldn't eat it. Actually, I couldn't even afford it, because at $19.50 (not including chips and drink), it was the most expensive sandwich I'd ever seen.

Until now. The deli sandwich that dazzled me couldn't hold a candle to the current record holder for high-priced eats.

The new champ is a half-eaten, ten-year-old grilled cheese job listed on eBay. As of this writing people have bid as much as $22,000 for this thing. And it's not because aged American cheese is a popular holiday choice.

The sandwich price is soaring because its owner, Diana Duyser, says it contains the image of the Virgin Mary.

I first saw the sandwich on TV. The sound was turned off but sure enough, I saw an image. I thought it was Marilyn Monroe. Must have been my Baptist upbringing. Duyser says she didn't realize her sandwich was special until after she took that first bite. Then she took a look and recoiled in horror as she realized she'd almost munched the Virgin Mary, an act which ranks right up there with making graven images as a sign of religious disrespect.

Frankly, I'm dubious about this one, even if the sandwich was made with Wonder Bread.

I'm not saying I don't believe in religious miracles. And I certainly believe folks are entitled to believe whatever they want.

But I believe this: if the good Lord had wanted to send a message to the world, He could have done better than a used sandwich from Fort Lauderdale, Florida.

I believe when God wants to get our attention, He'll do it up right. He'll appear in **BOLD PRINT**, in CAPITAL LETTERS, with quaking earth and raging seas and fire in the sky.

Speaking of which, the Bible tells us that when God wanted to tap Moses on the shoulder, He didn't send a message on a matzo ball. He set a bush on fire. God used a pillar of fire to lead the children of Israel through the wilderness. In the movie *The Ten Commandments*, when Charlton Heston held out his walking stick, God parted an entire sea.

Now that's making a statement. And ask yourself this: Moses came down from the mountain bearing two stone tablets containing God's Law. Would the children of Israel have been impressed if he had held up his hand and said, "If you look real close on this little wafer of manna, you can see..."?

But whether I'm a believer or not, these things continue to happen.

Years ago, traffic on an Atlanta interstate slowed to a crawl for days after a dude claimed he saw on a billboard the face of Jesus in a plate of spaghetti. Business at a barbecue joint boomed after a guy swore he'd seen the image of Malcolm X in a slab of ribs.

The saintly Florida sandwich set off some ugly copycat incidents. The Associated Press reports that soon after the Virgin Mary sandwich appeared, eBay pranksters posted two other sandwiches, one claiming to show the likeness of Mary's used chewing gum, the other depicting Mary Kate and Ashley Olsen. What's next, a bagel bearing the likeness of Moses?

Duyser said that at first she was "scared" of her sandwich. Then she realized its spiritual significance. Then she said, "I wanted to share it with the world."

Share it? For twenty-two thousand bucks?

Call me cynical, but if Duyser wants to do the right thing, she should look in the mirror and ask herself one question. Not "How much can I get?" but "What Would Mary Do?"

The Blighted Eye of the Beholder

Sir Isaac Newton earned certified "genius" status for developing the laws of modern physics, but even Newton had some help figuring out the laws of gravity. His inspiration was an apple falling from a tree, which prodded Newton to ask, "Wonder why that thing fell down instead of up?"

Sir Arthur Conan Doyle, who penned the Sherlock Holmes mysteries, openly admitted he cooked up some plots while high on cocaine. I read an autobiography of a famous painter who said he only felt inspired when he was naked.

Be it nakedness or falling fruit, the greats were all inspired by something.

Which brings us to Townsend Artman, who, according to the Associated Press, was inspired to pursue his form of "art" while driving his daughter to day care. Of course, what Artman calls art goes by other names in other places. At my house, we call it roadkill.

The "art" Artman discovered was a dead skunk on the road shoulder. Artman, who claims to earn a living as a wildlife photographer, says the sighting transformed him. Now, instead of shooting furry creatures romping through the forest primeval, he prefers animal still lifes, with the life involved being as still as it gets.

Artman seems to think there's no worse fate for an animal, and he places the blame squarely on man, saying, "It's a horrible thing to have happen to these animals, caught up in man's highway of death." Well, yes it is. Much better for them to perish in nature's "forest of death" where more animals are slaughtered each day by each other than will ever succumb to cars or trucks in the next decade.

Of course, while Artman deplores man's "highway of death," he hopes that portion of the road that runs by his place of business will be paved with gold as people clamor for his work.

But he admits that so far, his offerings haven't received widespread acceptance. Artman claims it's because the great, unwashed masses aren't savvy enough to recognize real art when they see it. I guess he means anyone who prefers gazing at the *Mona Lisa* instead of a postmortem possum is out of touch.

Frankly, I believe his public acceptance problem is a little more basic. Artman's asking price is $5,000 to $10,000 per piece, a little pricey for most folks, even for "normal" art.

Artman insists we just don't see his work in the proper perspective, saying he finds "...irony, humor, gruesomeness, beauty" in his subjects. It's been my experience that most of us, when we come across a fatally flattened critter, see (and smell) something else.

In the 1970s songwriter Loudon Wainwright III penned a classic called "Dead Skunk in the Middle of the Road," which was well received and still warmly remembered. I believe Loudon's lyrics sum up the general attitude toward roadkill.

This is America, and Artman is free to pursue his passion, but I wish he'd quit blaming the rest of us for his commercial failure as he seemed to be doing when he said, "There are a number of artists out there who are not mainstream...not everyone gets it."

I think Artman is missing the point entirely. The fact that folks aren't willing to shell out ten grand for a photo of roadkill doesn't mean they "don't get it."

I think it shows they get it perfectly.

Bad Eating Idea

For years I have placed myself in chiropractic peril by bending over backwards to accommodate the horde of Northerners who have flooded Georgia to take advantage of career opportunities, lovely weather and our renowned Southern hospitality.

I have stood idly by as they defiled our native tongue, gritting my teeth as their harsh, rough consonants rattled off the walls like linguistic BBs with each retelling of another gruesome, snow-related tale.

I have held my temper as they mocked our quaint Southern traditions with condescending comments about "how we did it up north."

I've endured it all. But no more. The Yankees are now attempting to tarnish our last unsullied icon of charm and gentility...Southern cooking.

I noticed this just the other day as I was surfing my expanded cable TV package. A new show claiming to feature "Great Southern Chefs" appeared, and I stopped to give it a look.

Before the first commercial aired, it was obvious the only thing "Southern" about this chef was the fact that he performed his gastronomic blasphemies at a restaurant in a neighboring Southern state.

Forget collards and cracklin' bread. When this dude smiled and introduced his dish of the day, it was not a Southern delight but some Pennsylvania Dutch atrocity called "scrapple."

It looked as noxious as its name implied. This scrapple stuff was a mixture of various ground and chopped meats (including liver), mashed together with buckwheat flour, cornmeal, spices, and other assorted goo and molded into a lump of something that can be most charitably described as "brown."

The mixture was then shoveled into loaf pans to sit in the refrigerator overnight, presumably to allow more time for this abomination to congeal into an even deadlier state.

The "chef" almost soiled himself explaining the various ways to eat scrapple, including frying and covering it with either syrup or half-cooked eggs.

He was still talking as I dashed for the Pepto-Bismol. I was disgusted that such a vile concoction would appear on a show dedicated to Southern cooking. Southern is black-eyed peas and hog jowl and barbecue and biscuits. Scrapple looked like something Satan would feed his pets.

Of course, I'm a tolerant kind of guy, and I say if Yankees want to eat scrapple, that's fine. As long as they eat it elsewhere. Georgia can do quite well without this culinary pestilence.

For the sake of our fine, untainted Southern children, I would like to see Georgia declared a scrapple-free state. Or barring that, at least require that scrapple eaters be licensed to consume this stuff within our sovereign borders.

To get a license, diners would first have to pass the Scrapple IQ Test. They could do so by producing either a Yankee driver's license or their day pass from the mental institution. Next, they would have to display a mastery of Southern cuisine. Not until a Northerner had whiffed the heavenly bouquet of boiled chitlins, swallowed a portion of pan-fried possum or savored that most provocative of Southern delicacies, the noble grit, would he or she be allowed to foul their digestive tract in my home state.

And if Yankees want to retaliate, that's fine. If they insist I pass a scrapple test before being allowed to savor Yankee foods, so be it. What would I be missing? Try finding a grit in Detroit. (Or a pulse, for that matter, but that's another story.)

I can live a full and happy life without ever swallowing a bite of such Northern delights as Cream of Wheat or Farina or Melba Toast. There's only one native Yankee food I ever liked, and thanks to modern refrigeration, I can get all the ice I want without ever leaving home.

No Balls at the UN

It was a beautiful mid-November day in Manhattan. Beneath crystal-blue skies, a brisk wind off the East River whipped the thicket of national flags lining the entrance plaza of the United Nations building.

In the sun-splashed UN sculpture garden, a crowd of red-faced guests giggled softly, occasionally pointing at the artwork they had come to see officially dedicated.

The new arrival was a sculpture of an animal, a gift to the UN from the art-rich nations of Kenya, Namibia and Nepal. As the crowd stood with teeth clenched to stifle the laughs, UN Secretary General Kofi Annan strode to the microphone, pointed with pride at the magnificent chunk of bronze, and in precise, clipped tones, said, "The sheer size of this creature humbles us. As well it should, for it reminds us that some things are bigger than we are."

Mr. Annan was probably not surprised that his remarks brought a chorus of chuckles from the crowd. Not because the sculpture was bad. It was good. In fact, the full-size likeness of an African bull elephant was perhaps a little too good.

You see, when the sculptor, a Bulgarian-born artist known only as Mihail, created the 11-foot-high work, he went to great lengths to insure a perfect likeness, going so far as to make a plaster cast of the creature from which to work.

The detail was astounding. Every wrinkle, every toenail, every curve of the tusk, bend of the trunk...everything. Right down to the elephant's most private part, all two feet of it.

Secretary General Annan's guests weren't the first to be impressed by the creature. The bronze behemoth had caused quite a stir even before its official unveiling. Motorists passing by on First Avenue had thoroughly enjoyed the magnificent display of elephant virility. One shouted, "Don't cut it off," another, "It's only natural."

It looks like their pleas for anatomical accuracy may fall on deaf ears. Despite the public's acceptance, even delight, in the beast, it looks like a little pruning of the elephant's privates may soon be ordered. Prior to Secretary General Annan's sculpture garden remarks, there were rumors that UN officials planned to take blowtorch in hand and reduce the elephant's organ to a less inflammatory size.

Indeed, shortly before the dedication ceremony, UN workers anxious to keep the crowd focused on Annan rather than the elephant had rearranged some large potted plants and small potted trees to screen viewers from the offensive appendage.

Advised of the potential desecration of his art, creator Mihail bubbled over in a testosterone-fueled frenzy. In a furious statement, he defended his sculpture's authenticity and scolded narrow-minded UN art Nazis, saying, "This is meant to be a symbol of all wildlife. You cannot castrate wildlife."

I'm sure thousands of gelding horses or polled Herefords or even run-of-the-mill steers would disagree, but sometimes it's hard to argue with an artist.

I'm hoping they find a solution short of pruning the priapic pachyderm. I'd suggest that for quick relief, the UN simply drop a few kudzu cuttings at the beast's feet. In a matter of days, the sculpture would resemble not so much an elephant as a leaf-draped double-wide.

But such a cover-up would probably not appease the UN's best and brightest. At least the males. Expect the boys of the foreign service corps to go on the offensive to make the massive member a memory.

It's a matter of self-esteem. The eunuchs masquerading as diplomats would probably feel threatened to have a man around the place who hadn't been emasculated.

Culinary Diversity

Three days after I graduated from high school, my father took me aside, grinned and said, "Guess what?"

Before I could, he finished. "I've found you a job. You start tomorrow. I'll take you to work. We leave at four in the morning."

A few hours later I was enjoying the sunrise on a dock in Grand Isle, Louisiana, waiting for the crew boat that would take me umpteen miles out in the Gulf of Mexico to wash dishes on an oil rig for the princely sum of $1.25 an hour.

It was delightful. I worked twelve-hour shifts for ten days straight, followed by five days of shore leave, a cycle which repeated itself all summer.

Life in the kitchen of Sea Drill #7 was amusing, entertaining, even. My boss was a retired Navy cook named Luce, who loved to expound on both his world travels and the several exotic strains of venereal disease he had managed to contract during his tenure with the fleet.

A young lad learns things during such adventures. I was no exception. When I wasn't washing dishes for 150 men or hauling frozen food from deck to deck, I was adding hundreds of colorful new curse words to my vocabulary, discovering how to make an alcoholic brew from raisins and absorbing oceans of info about cooking.

Well, at least about menu planning. Mostly, what to leave off. The roughnecks and roustabouts in our crew were not exactly cotillion material. They worked hard, cussed plenty and ate like they were raised in an orphanage. They were Cajuns.

The term "Cajun" is derived from the word "Acadian," the name of a group of French immigrants who, many, many years ago, repeatedly tried to settle in Canada and were repeatedly kicked out. After years of this, a few gained a toehold in the tundra and became official French Canadians. The smart ones said to heck with all that ice and snow, came south, settled in the bayous of south Louisiana and came to be known as Cajuns.

Cajuns are noted for many things, including a robust love of life and an absolute devotion to fine dining. It is said that a Cajun can make a meal out of anything worth eating. In addition to all manner of seafood, a Cajun will enjoy an occasional taste of raccoon and, when properly lubricated, will not hesitate to go eye-to-eye with a chitlin.

There are, however, certain foods a Cajun will not touch. At the top of the list is the muskrat, which Cajuns consider the fur-bearing spawn of Lucifer himself.

But amazingly, this rodent considered beyond redemption by the world's finest cooks is still appearing on certain dinner tables. Impossible, you say. If a Cajun won't eat it, who will?

Unfortunately... Yankees.

Specifically those of Acadian descent living in the Detroit area who are members of the Algonquin Club. Each year they gather to celebrate their French Canadian ancestry by boiling a batch of muskrat, which was a favorite of their fur-trapping Acadian forefathers.

Apparently the years of cold weather have taken their toll on the northern branch of the Acadian family tree. Their brains have finally frozen.

And my heart has melted. I normally don't issue an invitation like this, but in this case, it seems simply inhuman not to.

And so I say, please, come south, my frostbit brethren. Forsake your muskrat-munching ways and come to where the weather is warm and the people are sane and the only muskrat you'll see will be "napping" on the roadside, not nestled on your plate.

Join us. There's a place at the table just for you. You'll learn grits from gravy in no time, and with a little bit of luck, by this time next year, you'll be ready for possum.

A Chilling Spectacle

A grand affair for sure. The baby grand tinkles softly, conversation is a hushed murmur and candles flicker as attentive servers wave trays of canapés and chilled chardonnay among the guests. Another night, another opening in the art gallery world.

I don't know if the event attracted a major star, but it certainly had a theme. Possibly art for the end of the millenium. Maybe art for the end of the world, which may be where we're headed, judging by one of the show's offerings.

This gala was held in Bisbee, Arizona, not known as a hotbed of culture, but obviously a place where the occasional outrage can still get the juices flowing.

The source of all the fuss was a still life by budding artist Nicholas DeVore. At first glance the work seemed simple enough: a cloth-covered table dotted with napkins, chopsticks, soy sauce, flowers and teacups. At its center, a glass bowl ringed with fresh fruits and vegetables.

So far, so good. What's the big deal about a display of hors d'oeuvres and eating utensils? Why were some patrons upset over this innocuous work of art?

Maybe it had something to do with the frozen dead puppy that Nicholas gingerly placed in the middle of the glass bowl.

Yes, folks, Nicholas DeVore, self-styled artist and obvious fan of freeze-dried, took first place in the "Dogs At Large" show at Bisbee's Subway Gallery for putting a frozen dog on display.

You gotta give the boy credit. This was no spur-of-the-moment concoction. Nicholas had kept the puppy in his freezer for almost a year pending its artistic debut.

As you might expect, some of the show's patrons were disturbed to see a former Alpo consumer foisted upon them as a piece of art you could drive a nail with.

DeVore took offense at his critics, said his work was misunderstood. He defended his piece and said of its detractors: "They're typical squeamish American pet lovers that never looked death in the eye or don't have the perspective that it might be better to try and redeem the animal's short life rather than throw it in the trash can."

Translation: "You narrow-minded boors wouldn't recognize genius if it slapped you in the face. Especially if it's a frozen dog."

Count me among the Philistines. I'm still old-fashioned enough to prefer my art defrosted.

Not surprisingly, Nicholas has his defenders. One of them is Charles V. Hintner, an art professor at the University of Arizona and one of the three judges that awarded Nicky boy the grand prize for his efforts. Hintner said, "It was horrible in some ways, but very important."

Gallery board member Boyd Nicholl disagreed with the prof and vowed to wipe this slur from the eyes of Bisbee art lovers before too many of them had the chance to check out the Frozen Fido. "It won't be back," he said, meaning it would be gone the next day.

Indeed, it was. Devore took his centerpiece home to spend the evening in the old SubZero, and when he arrived to set up for the next day's showing, his entire display was gone, teacups and all, replaced by a small mound of dirt topped with a cross.

DeVore was devastated, saying, "It was like an art heist. They completely threw it all in the rubbish."

I guess that's where someone figured it belonged...in the rubbish.

He shouldn't be too upset. There's always a job out there for a boy with a creative mind and a thing for dragging corpses around. I might suggest that if Nick's art career ever hits the skids, he pursue his passion from another angle.

Dr. Death, aka Jack Kevorkian, who introduced America to assisted suicide, is not getting any younger. I'm sure he'll be needing an apprentice any day now.

Daring Dining Adventures

The weather was gloomy and so was I.

I needed a splash of brightness in my life. The Bahamas were out, but a new attraction in Manhattan looked perfect.

In early February, an artist named Christo, aided by his fuchsia-headed wife, Jeanne-Claude, erected something called "The Gates" in New York's Central Park. The gates are basically 7,500 sets of brightly painted goalposts lining the park's miles of trails.

From each frame hangs a big, bright, cheery piece of fabric. It looked like fun, and I decided to make a one-day trip to the Big Apple just to check it out. But when I called several major (and minor) airlines, the lowest of their "low, low, impossibly low" fares was still too much.

So I stayed home. At first, I was sad. Not anymore.

Every time I'm in New York I try a new restaurant. With my luck, had I gone to see Christo's "work," I would have wound up at the trendy new midtown eatery offering "clothing-optional" dining. In other words, a chance to eat naked.

This is wrong in so many ways I don't know where to start.

I realize some people get a kick out of going naked. And it's fine with me if they want to hang out together, but I don't want them hanging out where I'm trying to eat—no matter how fashionable their accessories are.

Reuters News Agency sent a reporter to cover the uncovered action. The reporter interviewed diner George Keyes, 65, who said he was a retired English teacher. I hope he didn't teach in the same outfit he wore to dinner, which included earrings, a necklace and something made from black leather with attractive red studs. It was called a "genital bracelet." Just the name is enough to make you lose your lunch.

Besides being a showcase for bad fashion, the naked nibbling experience seems like a potential health risk. The only time I ever ate naked was at Boy Scout camp after the older scouts stole my clothes. I picked up two ticks and a red bug.

At a naked restaurant, there's no telling what you might pick up...or come down with. You don't know what people might be shedding other than their clothes. Diners were told to bring something to sit on, like a towel.

People used to make jokes about catching "social diseases" off toilet seats in the bus station. Try telling your loved one you caught something off the plush chair at the naked restaurant. In the old days, a hair in your soup almost certainly came from the kitchen. In this scenario, it could have come from anywhere. I hope it's not considered cheating to keep a napkin in your lap.

And what about body parts? Not all of us are lean, mean hardbodies. What happens if a full-figured woman leans over her linguini or accidentally slops over into the salad bowl? Sorry, but at a restaurant the only things I want to see dangling are stray participles on the menu.

The windows were papered over to protect passing pedestrians, and servers were required by the health code to be fully clothed, so at least the public couldn't see the goings-on at the invitation-only gathering, and that's a blessing. Even in New York, some things should be kept behind closed doors.

There are lots of things you should do naked, including taking a bath. There are lots of things you should not do naked. At the top of the list is going out to eat.

I like my steak rare, but not raw. I like my fellow diners the same way... the rawer they are, the more rarely I like to see them.

On the bright side, you don't have to worry about getting a spot on your tie.

TAMING THE WILD, WILD WEST

I was 54 years old before I made it to Montana.

It was worth the wait.

Dog Days Disappearing in America

During the so-called Age of Enlightenment, a self-anointed wise man opined that a society could be judged by the way it treated its weakest members. Hogwash. Such tripe may fly with the Save-The-Whale types, but any fool knows a society is best judged by the way it treats its dogs.

Several years ago I finally threw a bag in the car and headed for Key West, spurred by rumors that Hemingway's former haunt was in danger of becoming as plasticized as the rest of Florida. I wanted to see the place before all traces of its legendary charm were buried beneath the Golden Arches.

It was everything I'd hoped for...quirky, funny, offbeat and laid back. The drive down was long and hot, and as soon as the bags were unpacked I headed out in search of a cool drink. The bar on a back street in Old Town was packed with decidedly un-touristy types and something even better... dogs.

To get from the bar to a table you had to dodge the owner's passel of mutts, who were scattered around the outdoor deck like so many lumpy carpets.

It was lovely.

Last year's trip to Britain ended with a family gathering at a remote village in the Highlands of Scotland. The celebration's hub was the Loch Duich Hotel, an eight-room, no-star joint long on charm and local color and overseen by Ian, the owner, along with his wife and children and their dog, Brodie.

When he wasn't schmoozing snacks from patrons in the bar or dining room, the chocolate lab wandered wherever he pleased, including the rooms of unsuspecting guests. It was clear that anyone who couldn't tolerate Brodie was welcome to leave.

I can't wait to go back.

Which brings me to Montana. I'm headed that way in a few weeks for a few days. It's just another of those places I promised I'd see but still haven't, and now that Montana has been discovered by the "beautiful people," it seems wise to check it out before the Ted Turners and Tom Cruises of the world transform the Big Sky state into Hollywood North or Cowboy World.

The flight was booked a few weeks ago, and originally, my travel agenda consisted solely of renting a car and driving around at random, gulping down what sights I could in a few days and stopping at any place that looked interesting. But now, I may have to add a haircut to the itinerary. At least if I can get it at Ed Dutton's barbershop in Kalispell. Last week, a story about Dutton came across the Associated Press wire. The Montana dateline caught my eye, but Dutton's story stole my heart.

Chances are Dutton doesn't cut hair any better than the next fellow with a striped pole, but I'm not going for the barbering. I'm hoping to see Coco, Dutton's Springer Spaniel. For years now, as Dutton has shorn the skulls of countless cowboys (and possibly even an Indian or two), Coco has been a fixture in the shop, snoozing the day away beneath a blizzard of hair clippings.

No one ever complained, but a few weeks ago a bureaucrat from the Montana Board of Barbers came in, saw the dog, fined the barber $500 and said the pooch had to go. Once the incident became public, a furor ensued, and after receiving hundreds of petitions in support of Dutton, the Board of Barbers is reconsidering its ban on barbershop dogs.

A good sign, but just in case the ban holds, I want to see Ed Dutton for myself. He may not be much of a barber, but any man who likes his dog that much can't be all bad.

By the way, a recent news report from Key West says a city ordinance has been proposed that would ban dogs from public buildings, including restaurants and bars. Made it just in time.

I leave for Montana in mid-September. Hope I'm not too late.

Gone West, Part 1

When I booked the trip to Montana, the World Trade Towers were still standing, the Braves were still playing baseball, and the hot topic in Washington was how to spend a dwindling surplus. It was business as usual across the board, an ideal time to get away for a few days, meet some new people and take some bad photos of what I'd heard was some of the most gorgeous scenery on earth.

The original trip was canceled by a group of lunatics who decided the way to honor their god was to kill a few thousand innocent people, but by mid-October, the skies were friendly once more, so I gave it another try.

Three hours sandwiched in a middle seat from Atlanta to Denver was a study in travel hell, but the two-hour hop to Montana seemed too short. The small commuter jet banked north on takeoff, offering a first glimpse of the Rocky Mountains, spread out below like a wrinkled blanket sprinkled with confectioners' sugar. Farther north the snow cover grew thicker, sifting down into the upper valleys of Yellowstone and the lower reaches of Montana's Bitterroots.

The walk across the tarmac from the plane to the terminal in Missoula was windy and cold, but the rental car was waiting as promised, heater purring away. I headed north, away from what passes for civilization in that part of the world, hoping to get a taste of the back country before the sun set.

I once wrote that before God built hell, He practiced on West Texas. He must have warmed up for heaven by doing Montana. Pictures don't begin to do the place justice. Pictures don't show how the mountains change color from minute to minute as the sun rolls across the sky, moving from a backlit gold at sunrise to steely gray at noon to soft pewter as the sun fades at day's end.

The pictures can't tell you how a single fall day in the mountain valleys can find you driving through rain, snow, clouds and splashes of sunshine so bright two pair of shades aren't enough.

I stopped at the first town past the two grazing buffalo. Arlee was a small clump of run-down stores, including one advertising Native American crafts guaranteed to please any tourist (especially one from Georgia who wouldn't know a Native American rug from a Martha Stewart toilet seat cover).

The shop was closed. The summer tourist season had officially ended two days earlier, and the roads wouldn't be filled with artifact-seeking strangers again until after Thanksgiving, when the ski resorts opened.

I drove across the street to a gas station and bought some high-priced petrol and a pack of crackers and said hello to the Indians inside, who gave me back only silence and sullen stares.

A few miles down the road, it dawned on me that I'd been too busy watching the distant mountains to notice the shacks and mobile homes along Highway 93 that passed for first-class living on the Flathead Indian Reservation.

I drove on to Polson, a three-stoplight town at the south end of Flathead Lake. Forty-two dollars got me a lake-view room complete with kitchenette and a storm door thick enough to stop bullets. I dropped the bags off, washed up and headed for the Salish Point Marina and Casino for dinner, hoping to meet some locals and finally get a taste of the real Montana.

Three of the "regulars" were there, hungry enough for new faces to buy me a free beer. I said thanks and, not knowing what else to talk about, inquired about the weather. They smiled and asked for another round of drinks. I was about to learn that in Montana, talking about the weather takes a while.

Gone West, Part 2 — Talking With the Veterans

The bar at the Salish Point Marina and Casino in Polson, Montana, was an L-shaped affair that ran from the door of the attached Chinese restaurant to a dimly lit room where video gambling machines flickered and flashed as they gobbled loose change from a handful of customers.

Three local guys occupied the short end of the bar, and I took a seat halfway down the long leg, between the locals and an Indian woman nursing a beer and a hangover.

Kathy walked up, smiled and asked if I wanted a drink. I pointed at the glass of foamy brown liquid in front of the man two seats away and said, "Give me one of those."

Before Kathy had cracked the bottle of Alaskan Amber, the man farthest from me tipped his cowboy hat, told Kathy the beer was on him and asked where I was from. My answer brought a giggle from the middle of the three men, who immediately produced a dirty postcard featuring a lewdly posed, half-naked woman he described as a "Georgia peach."

I grimaced at the card and mumbled a couple of words and he announced the next beer was on him because he liked the way I talked. I used my next few syllables of Southern-ese to inquire about weather. Four inches of snow were predicted for the mountains that night and it was already below freezing in Polson, and I mentioned it seemed awful cold for October.

The guys chuckled and spent the better part of two beers telling me not to worry, that Flathead Lake, on whose shores we were seated, kept the temperature "moderate" all winter, rarely dropping to more than 10 below zero. Max, sitting next to me, said you didn't have to worry until the thermometer hit 30 below, at which point your feet were likely to freeze to the pavement if you didn't keep moving along.

With my Southern blood running colder by the minute, I tried to steer the conversation to something a little warmer, like the war on terrorism.

The three were all Navy combat veterans of different wars. The two older guys had spent their time on ships at sea and didn't have much to offer. Max, who had served two tours in Vietnam running counterinsurgency operations from a boat in the Mekong River, said things would be fine in Afghanistan as long as we let the military run the operations.

"Politicians took over in Vietnam, and that's when I got out," he said. Getting out for Max meant coming back to Montana and traveling for a Montgomery, Alabama-based company until he patented a piece of equipment that left him comfortable enough to live and work where and when he wanted—which was in Montana, and part-time.

Nobody seemed to have any hard feelings against the Muslims, though, not even Max, who was the only Jew in Lake County as far as he knew and had to drive 70 miles to Missoula to attend Sabbath services in a "synagogue" disguised as the basement of a Protestant church.

"Muslims don't bother me," he said. "Besides, there's no time to think about that. The army can do the fighting. I've got to get ready for winter."

The firewood was long since stacked, but Max was worried about his plums. The bears had already started raiding the trees in his front yard, not two miles away across the lake. "Saw a grizzly in there this morning," he said.

With that, he and the others explained that the best way for me to see Montana was to ditch the rental car, hire a horse and head for the high country. "Liable to see a bear that way, if you're lucky."

We shook hands in the parking lot, lied about keeping in touch and split. *Cowboys, Indians and bears in just one day*, I thought. *This is turning out better than planned.* With each passing hour, Montana seemed more and more like another world.

In the next two days, it would start to seem a lot more like home.

Gone West, Part 3 — Home is Where ... Ever

The first full day in Montana dawned dreary but full of promise. In less than twenty-four hours, I'd encountered genuine cowboys and Indians and heard stories about backyard bears. I couldn't wait to see what would happen next.

Day two was designated as "scenic drive" day, which meant Glacier National Park, the top pick on everybody's "must-see" list in northwest Montana.

I went by way of Big Fork, mostly because a woman from Chicago I met on the plane from Denver told me her friend in Montana had said Big Fork was a "fabulous," authentic Western frontier town.

Big Fork was about as authentic as Dollywood, an assortment of log (and faux-log) buildings, including a little ski-resort type "village" filled with cute shops featuring Native American trinkets and Western memorabilia, most of which were made in Taiwan.

I put Big Fork in the rearview and headed on to Glacier, anxious to travel Going-to-the-Sun Road all the way to the Continental Divide at Logan Pass.

The Ranger at the park entrance told me overnight snows had closed the road eight miles short of Logan Pass, but I was welcome to go as far as I could then loop back. I'd driven 70 miles that morning to see the place, so I paid 10 bucks to make what amounted to a 40-mile U-turn.

Glacier was as spectacular as advertised, but spending less than an hour in a national park twice the size of Rhode Island seemed, well ... stupid.

Noon came and I figured the town of Hungry Horse was a logical spot for lunch. It probably had been three days earlier when the town's only restaurant was open. It was now closed until ski season, like most everything else. I ate at the two-booth café attached to the gas station then headed to Whitefish to see how the recent invasion of Hollywood types had affected what was reputed to have once been a picturesque little town.

Whitefish was worse than Big Fork and appeared to have been renovated by the editors of *Ski Cliché Digest*. It was Gatlinburg with cappuccino instead of cold beer. The local movie theater was hosting a poetry reading.

Cappuccino and poetry I could get back home, so I pushed on to Kalispell and holed up at the circa-1900 Grand Hotel, touted as one of the town's "historic treasures."

Except for the giant motel and casino that looked like it had been transplanted from Biloxi, Kalispell was cute and quaint and almost managed to exude some frontier flavor. Until I noticed the car in the hotel parking lot with Lowndes County, Georgia, license plates.

The next day I drove back to Missoula to spend the last two nights and one day of my dream trip. I wound up at a Holiday Inn that was hosting a bunch of Birkenstock-shod health care professionals who were discussing not frostbite—as I would have expected—but diabetes.

Reserve Street was littered with the same assortment of fast-food joints and chain stores found in Anywhere Else, U.S.A., but downtown Missoula was a little different. In less than six blocks I saw bikers, joggers and homeless panhandlers, all bundled up like Eskimos. It was like a heavily layered version of Miami.

I drove to Idaho and back just to say I'd been there and spent the last night of my dream vacation at the bar of the Missoula Holiday Inn, watching the only black man I'd seen in three days run across the big screen TV in a U. of Montana football jersey. The guy next to me asked the bartender to find something else on the small TV behind the beer tap.

In seconds the screen flickered, the Atlanta Braves appeared, and the guy next to me said, "All right!" When he told me he was from Atlanta, I knew it was time to leave.

Thomas Wolfe once said, "You can't go home again." These days, it seems like no matter how hard you try, you can't leave home behind.

CULTURE WARS, CULTURE SHOCK

Once upon a time you had to travel to a foreign country
to see how the rest of the world lived. Now, you don't have to
leave your neighborhood. Bringing cultures together is
a good thing, but bridging the diversity gap can be messy.

A Lifetime of Nonsense

I'm eating a chili dog and doing some absentminded channel surfing when this gorgeous woman appears on the screen. I drop the clicker and watch. She's walking through a leafy glade, the sky is clear and blue, and the surf mutters at the nearby shore. Then, slowly, she turns to the camera and begins to deliver an earnest monologue...about her lifelong struggle with yeast infections.

Yikes! I dropped the chili dog and checked the channel. Lifetime—The Channel For Women. I should have known. You can't surf past Lifetime without seeing some (happy-faced, teary-eyed, pimple-covered)...(girl, young lady, old woman)...(moaning, weeping, cheering) about constipation, water retention, bloating, cramps, incontinence or other topics too delicate to mention here.

On Lifetime they regularly advertise pads, potions, powders, pills and all manner of products to cure all manner of female ailments. Lifetime is enough to make me happy to be a guy, thankful I'm not the target of ads for anything more serious than hair loss.

Or I wasn't until recently.

The other day I was cruising through town, listening to the radio, when a female voice came on. It tickled a memory, and I thought, Wow, it's the girl from Lifetime ! They're gonna run a yeast infection spot on an all-sports station!

I was amazed. I was also wrong. No yeast in this ad. The sultry-voiced woman was pitching a set of products designed to enhance a man's sexual performance. And I'm not talking Viagra here.

This stuff takes over once Viagra has kicked in. The ad was appalling. From the use of terms like "increased payload" and "staying power," I might have thought the announcer chick was describing a long bed pickup truck or a new antiperspirant.

Then she purred that her miracle potion would turn the meekest male into a sexual sabertooth who could "go all night."

Frankly, the last time I used the term "go all night," I was describing a pesky bladder condition to my doctor. This ad had something else in mind entirely.

It disturbed me. And I'm no prude. I was the first kid to sneak a copy of the Sears & Roebuck catalog on a scout camping trip so we could all look at the dirty pictures in the underwear section. I was also voted best kisser in the eighth grade. I'm no prude, but this was too much.

Being a guy used to be easy. A cave man went out and killed something to eat. The old lady cooked it and after supper, if the man was in the mood, he performed his reproductive duties while the cave babe did her nails or picked her toes.

The modern feminist movement ruined all that. After years of faking it, women demanded the right to actually enjoy sex. Worst of all, they decided it was a good idea to actually tell their partners what they liked and what they didn't.

And if that ad for the miracle sexual potion is correct, it sounds like things have reached a point where women are now scoring their men like Olympic athletes.

"Earl, your artistic expression was good, but you had some problems there with your technique. The triple twist with a half-gainer was nice, but your dismount was a little weak. Best I can give you is a 6.5."

Frankly, this is pressure I don't need. I don't want women discussing me like I'm a high (or low) performance sports car.

Mercifully, I'm in a stage of reproductive dormancy at the moment. But if I wasn't, and I was thinking of entering the "love zone" again, I wouldn't know what to do first—have my fluids checked...or my head.

Tacky, Even for Texas

Since this year's vacation will be taking place in my dreams, the list of possible destinations should be endless. Sadly, it's not. After running across an article in the *New York Times*, Lajitas, Texas, is definitely out of the running.

It's a shame, really. Sounds as if once upon a time, Lajitas was my kind of place. Small, quiet, peaceful, too remote for cell phones and almost 300 miles from a major airport. But last spring, Lajitas lost its appeal for me. Hard to pull for a town that allows its mayor to be publicly castrated.

Normally, I wouldn't be so squeamish about an elected official being treated in this manner. But this politician is different. The mayor of Lajitas is a beer-drinking goat.

His name is Clay Henry III, and he is the third in his family to hold the highest (and only) elected office in Lajitas. The original Clay Henry was elected in the seventies. He was followed in office by Clay Henry Jr. and, in 2000, by Clay Henry III, who won election handily despite being opposed by a wooden Indian and a dog named Clyde.

Since there's no City Hall, Clay Henry III does his beer drinking and hanging out at the Lajitas Trading Post. And that's the problem. So does everyone else, especially the new arrivals—the artists, yuppies and land speculators who have flocked to Lajitas in recent years, drawn by its wild beauty and relatively low dirt prices.

One of them is a wealthy Houstonian who bought a spread in Lajitas to use as a weekend retreat. He was having it remodeled by a couple of non-local guys who stayed in the house while they worked.

Last April the two nail drivers were perched in front of the Trading Post when a car drove up bearing another rich out-of-towner and his hot date, whom the guy was looking to impress.

The rich guy figured showing his chick how Clay Henry could pound a beer would do the trick, but there was a problem. The rich guy didn't have a beer, and since it was Sunday morning, the Trading Post was closed. But the two workmen were there, along with their overflowing cooler.

The rich dude in the fancy car asked the good old boys if he could borrow a beer. They said sure, thinking the man was gonna drink it. Then they watched in horror as the dude snapped the cap off a Heineken and popped the bottle into the thirsty mouth of Clay Henry, who promptly turned up the beer and drank it down.

The out-of-town contractors were not aware of Clay Henry's status in the community and took great offense at the mayor's actions. One of them showed his displeasure by whipping out a pocketknife and castrating Clay Henry on the spot.

The rescue squad managed to save the goat's life but not his gonads, which the boozing butcher had taken along as a souvenir. When word of the mutilation spread, it was all Brewster County Sheriff Ronnie Dodson could do to maintain order. "They wanted to lynch the guy," said Dodson. "Clay Henry is an institution in West Texas."

Thankfully, the *Times* article reports that Clay Henry III is now wholly recovered, if not quite whole, and boozing it up again, this time to ease his pain rather than get a buzz.

Hilton Head, Key West, Destin and now Lajitas. Once again the beautiful people have ruined a perfectly good place, which means my search for a dream vacation spot continues.

If I ever find that dream spot, I promise two things. First, that in honor of Clay Henry III, I'll buy the mayor a beer. Second, that in hopes of keeping the place perfect, I'll never tell a soul.

This Idea is All Wet

"And so by the powers vested in me by the creators of Star Trek and the owners of Sea World, I now pronounce you...woman and fish."

Can't happen? Just did.

Imagine trying to sell Hollywood a script about a woman who marries a dolphin. They'd laugh you right off Sunset Boulevard.

But it just happened when the lovely, talented and mentally suspect Ms. Sharon Tendler flew to Israel and—on the shores of the fabled Red Sea—tied the knot with the love of her life, a 35-year-old male dolphin inappropriately named Cindy.

After the vows were exchanged, the 41-year-old bride said, "I'm the happiest girl on Earth. I made a dream come true, and I am not a pervert."

Certainly not. She's just nuts. But in her defense, Tendler has made a career of hanging out with a rather "eccentric" crowd.

Tendler became a self-made millionairette producing rock concerts in her native England. She spent some of the money vacationing in exotic places, including Dolphin Reef resort in Eilat, Israel.

Tendler claims she got the hots (or wets) for Cindy 15 years ago. Since then she has flown to Eilat two or three times a year to splash with her sweetie. (Cindy did not travel to England because of nagging visa problems.)

As time passed, Tendler's love for Cindy grew. Unfortunately her IQ did not, which may explain this Tendler comment:

"The peace and tranquility underwater, and his love, would calm me down."

Cheaper than Valium, I guess. But I digress.

Finally, unable to contain her love for Flipper any more, Tendler went to Cindy's trainer, Maya Zilber, who is fluent in fish and agreed to ask Flipper how he felt about hooking up with a human.

(And yes, I know a dolphin is technically a mammal, but for my money, if its day job is swimming in the ocean and eating other fish, it's a fish. Period.)

After extended consultation, Zilber told Tendler Cindy was thrilled at the idea of marrying a landlocked loony.

When word of the proposed wedding surfaced, Tendler was pelted with questions about how she fell in love—and why.

"It's not a bad thing," she said. "It's just something that we did because I love him, but not in the way that you love a man. It's just a pure love that I have for this animal."

A pure love Tendler intended to pursue to the end of the rainbow. Or at least the edge of the Red Sea. And so it was that on Thursday, December

29, 2005, the big event occurred.

Tendler wore a white wedding dress and pink flowers in her hair. Cindy wore a natty sharkskin vest. After a brief ceremony on a floating dock, the woman pledged her undying love to the fish. Then she kissed him and tossed him a mackerel. Really.

Tendler's friends threw her in the ocean to join her new hubby.

The couple did not disclose plans for an extended honeymoon, but Tendler said they would spend their wedding night "going bowling." Really.

Normally, I'd say what a waste. But considering all the unattractive (not to mention possibly illegal) alternatives, bowling may be a blessing.

And what if things don't work out?

Tendler insists they will and went so far as to call herself a "one-dolphin woman." But when pressed by reporters, she also said she retains the option of "marrying human."

And to think people were outraged in 1957 when rock and roll legend Jerry Lee Lewis married his 13-year-old cousin.

Times have certainly changed. For the better? Let's talk it over on our next fishing trip.

Say Amen, Brother

Too bad the personal travel budget is so tight. Otherwise, I'd cruise up to suburban Richmond, Virginia, to attend the next meeting of the Chesterfield County Board of Supervisors.

It ought to be quite an occasion. Especially the "invocation."

In the past, the board has opened for business with a word of prayer, offered by representatives of universally recognized religions, including Judaism, Christianity and Islam.

That's about to change. Thanks go to Cyndi Simpson, who recently decided the board's religious choices weren't inclusive enough and went to court for the right to offer the opening prayer on behalf of her religion.

Cyndi Simpson is a practitioner of Wicca. She's a witch.

The suit was filed on Simpson's behalf by the American Civil Liberties Union and some outfit called the Americans United for Separation of Church and State, although in this case, the lawsuit doesn't seem to be aimed so much at separating church and state as making sure every religion, no matter how obscure, gets a shot at some government-sanctioned publicity.

That Wicca has been recognized as an official religion by Chesterfield County, Virginia, isn't surprising. It could happen anywhere. But it does raise an interesting question. Namely, when Cyndi Simpson gets up to pray, to whom will she address herself?

Most prayers I've heard open with a plea for attention (or mercy) from God or Jesus or Allah. But it looks like Cyndi Simpson's options are virtually limitless.

A recent news report about the Chesterfield incident said, "Wicca is regarded as a natural religion, grounded in the earth. Followers of its many different forms generally believe all living things, as well as stars, planets, and rocks, have a spirit."

If that isn't confusing enough, the wicca.com website muddies matters further with this: "...when invoking the Goddess and God... it is a personal preference and what a Witch uses depends on what 'feels' right for them individually."

Sounds like Simpson could ask for guidance from the Cosmic Muffin or the spirit of my deceased dog, Biscuit, and claim she's getting the job done.

Frankly, this is disturbing. When government bodies are allegedly engaged in the responsible expenditure of tax dollars, I hate to think they start their business by invoking the wisdom of the ficus plant in the foyer.

When I myself seek divine guidance, I hope to get the attention of something or someone more omnipotent than a piece of gravel in the driveway or the can of potted meat in the pantry.

But according to Wiccan tradition, anything goes.

The pro-witch ruling was made by U.S. District Court Judge Dennis W. Dohnal, who said Chesterfield County's traditional opening prayer denied Simpson her constitutional right of free expression of her religious beliefs. The 47-year-old Simpson said she hoped Dohnal's ruling would help bring credibility to witchcraft as a religion.

Well, sure. Nothing like a court ruling in your favor to restore credibility. Just ask O.J. Simpson.

It's too late to turn back the clock on this one, but I wonder if the judge or the witch has considered the far-reaching implications of the ruling. Consider this: if Simpson opens a meeting by invoking the spirit of the Great Cockroach in the Sky, how, in good conscience, could the board of supervisors proceed with renewing the pest control contract on the county courthouse, knowing they would be sentencing to death the very creatures that blessed their gathering to begin with?

Of course there are occasions when a Wiccan prayer would be appropriate. Like maybe Halloween. Or Earth Day. Or if the board's agenda included a vote on the expansion of the local sewer plant. With all the extra B.S. headed Chesterfield County's way, it's a sure bet that one's gonna be coming up soon.

A Step in the Wrong Direction

You look for the small things...the cracks and fissures and breaks that indicate something has changed...and not necessarily for the better.

Sometimes I watch MTV. Most times I wish I hadn't. But if what I saw the other day was indicative of future trends, this nation is doomed.

I'm not talking about the impending war with Iraq, or global warming or declining dolphin populations. What I saw recently was proof of the corruption of our modern youth. And what I saw was—teenage boys dancing.

Worse, they looked like they enjoyed it. Granted, it wasn't much to look at and what passed for dancing looked like a lab experiment where people had been wired to something and were being intermittently electrocuted. But the boys were definitely moving to what passed for a beat...and they were doing it by the bunch...and with smiles on their faces.

Teenage boys? Dancing? This is madness.

A society has to draw the line somewhere, and in the past, American men have drawn that line very clearly. Ballroom dancing, also known as "slow dancing," has always been an acceptable behavior for young men because it involves an embrace of some sort and is really an excuse for guys to grope a chick without getting slapped.

And male ballet dancers certainly have their place in the art world, as do the guys who fling themselves across the stage during Broadway dance numbers, like those in *West Side Story*, featuring dances that are essentially choreographed combat, with guys getting punched or stabbed in the grand finale. Really cool.

Male folk and square dancers and even those who prance to the polka are acceptable, if somewhat disturbing. But recreational dancing between boys and girls to hit music? You're asking for trouble. French kids did the minuet three hundred years ago and look where that excuse for a country is today.

This is not only not cool...it is also unbiblical.

Anyone who has ever seen the movie *The Ten Commandments* knows that in biblical times the only people who danced were women, and the only women who danced were painted hussies who only shook themselves in order to inflame the passions of men while the story line of the movie moved from plagues and pestilence to battle scenes filled with hot, sweaty men who were mostly fighting to get rid of excess testosterone that accumulated while they were watching the hussies dance the night before.

This goes back to the dawn of mankind. Cave drawings don't show pictures of sock hops. The only time cavemen danced was to celebrate a manly achievement...like killing a sabertooth tiger or the guy in the cave next door.

It may have been the Stone Age, but mixed couples did not rock.

If young boys absolutely must dance, they should keep it to themselves. My buddies and I accomplished this at Boy Scout meetings, when we paid tribute to our Native American ancestors by doing what our Scout leaders told us were "authentic" Indian dances. They were probably about as authentic as instant grits, but we chanted and shuffled and we got rid of that dancing urge without doing any harm to our self-esteem, or our public image.

When I was in high school, guys were so unskilled at the unmanly art, an entire song was created just to encourage boys to boogie. This was accomplished by including the dance steps in the lyrics of the song, which went like this...

"You put your left foot in,
You take your left foot out,
You put your left foot in,
And you shake it all about.
You do the Hokey Pokey
And turn yourself about
That's what it's all about..."

Speaking of which...it may be hokey, but our young men need to be reminded—and right now—that no matter what may happen on MTV, when it gets right down to it...

Real guys don't dance.

Scary Stuff for School Kids

I didn't have to check the calendar to realize summer was officially over. My place backs up to the playground of one of the local kindergartens, and when school is in session, the playground is a beehive of activity. It's wonderful to hear the squeals and screams of delight as the children romp and play all day long.

Nice to see some things don't change. When I attended kindergarten, recess was the highlight of the school day, too. My school housed grades K-6, and we had recess twice a day. The teachers turned us all loose at once, and when we hit the playground it was a free-for-all.

The kids at the kindergarten behind me love to ride their Big Wheel scooters at recess, but the big wheels at my school were the sixth graders. They made the playground rules, the main rule being that sixth graders ruled.

Sometimes, they would go out of their way to make us little kids miserable. They'd stomp on the sand forts we crafted for our marble shooing. They'd steal our red rubber dodge ball and hog the slides and swings. They lived to torment us. But on those rare days they left us alone, that playground was magical. On that sandy stretch I ran races, chased girls and broke my arm for the first time. It was fabulous.

But even better than recess was the walk home. The two-car household was nonexistent in those days, at least among my circle of friends. Each family had one car, and the man of the house drove it to work. So in the morning, when time was short, I rode the bus to school with my friend Danny.

But in the afternoon, with all the time in the world to get home, we walked. And those walks were always an adventure. Even when the older kids came along.

I revisited the old neighborhood recently and clocked the route from the school to my former house at about two miles. Back then, it seemed endless. Especially the block where the haunted house sat.

We could have made a short detour and avoided the house, but we rarely did. It was old, with peeling paint and broken windows and waist-high weeds in the yard. We never saw anyone there, but the older kids had an endless supply of stories about the place. About the ghostly noises that could be heard there at night and about the crazy man who lived in the attic and preyed on little kids.

Sometimes, the sixth graders would actually go into the house and brag about their boldness, taunting us for being chicken. Didn't matter. All the taunting in the world couldn't have gotten us into that house.

It was terrifying at the time, but looking back, passing that scary old house made it that much better to get back to the comfort and safety of home. That creepy old bungalow made those walks home wonderful. And memorable.

I wish the kids at the kindergarten behind me could experience the same kind of walking-home adventures. But they don't. Without exception they leave school via bus or carpool.

I once thought the parents of the kids who lived close enough to walk home were doing them a disservice by driving them home. Now I know better. With kidnappings and child molesters in the news almost daily, letting a kid walk home, even in the best neighborhoods, is like playing roulette with a human life.

How tragic. I'm glad those kids behind me still have recess. I'm just sorry they don't get to experience the childhood magic of a long walk home.

I'm sorry, but I understand. These days, the bad guys in the haunted house are liable to be real.

Cold-blooded Violence

Look hard enough, you'll find a silver lining in any cloud. Right now, the good news on the campaign front is that the presidential candidates aren't talking about gun control. This probably means polls indicate gun control is the last thing on voters' minds. But it could indicate the candidates have finally figured out that when people intend to harm one another, they'll find a way to do it.

My mother is a prime example. She was from the "Spare the rod and spoil the child" school of discipline, and every time I strayed she walloped me with whatever was at hand.

One day, she caught me copping a fresh-baked cookie before supper. This was a major no-no. Mother had left her favorite switch outside but decided I needed immediate attention and grabbed the first thing she saw—her yardstick.

Unfortunately for me, the puny little stick broke on the first whack, causing my sister to laugh and infuriating mother even more. She turned my rear end red with a spatula.

I never looked at homemade cookies the same way again but later realized that mother was following well-established biblical precedent regarding the creative use of weapons.

Cain performed the first recorded murder when he slew his brother, Abel. Cain didn't have a Colt .45, a baseball bat or even a hockey stick. All he had was a rage and a rock. That's all he needed.

David didn't have a semi-automatic assault weapon, so he whacked Goliath with a stone and a slingshot. When Samson still had his hair, he slew his enemies with the jawbone of an ass.

It's been a while since ass jawbones have shown up in a police report, but folks are still getting the job done. And they're more creative than ever.

I still recall a bizarre case of domestic violence in Pennsylvania. I don't remember why the husband got so mad at his wife, but I do remember that when the dude lost control, he didn't have a gun.

No problem. He simply went to the freezer and grabbed a frozen turkey and proceeded to beat his old lady with a Butterball. The turkey eventually softened, but the man's heart didn't. His wife was still conscious so the guy went back to the freezer and got a pound of frozen ground round, with which he finished the beating—and his wife.

At the time, I said that if gun control advocates were serious about saving lives, they should demand a ban on frozen foods. Maybe the ban should expand to include live reptiles, which are the weapon of choice of Mr. David Havenner of Port Orange, Florida.

A recent Associated Press story says Havenner and his live-in love interest, Nancy Monico, had been having issues. The tension led to trouble and the trouble led to violence and cops rushed to the scene.

What they saw shocked them.

Monico was bruised and battered as expected. But the manner in which she had been mauled was what stunned the cops. Monico said when the fight started, Havenner was content to pound her with his fists. But when that didn't satisfy him, he started pelting her with beer bottles.

Monico tried to flee. Havenner followed, swinging his weapon of last resort...the three-foot alligator that lived in the bathtub of the couple's mobile home. After several misses, Havenner finally managed to make contact with Monico. The blow from the gator knocked Monico senseless and left the reptile reeling.

When questioned by the cops, Havenner claimed it wasn't his fault at all. He said Monico started the fight when she bit him on the arm. Havenner said she was agitated because the couple had run out of booze.

Ban guns? Nice idea, but if we've reached a point where people are being assaulted with alligators, what we need to ban isn't guns but idiots.

I won't hold my breath.

Trouble Under the Sheets

"Good evening, brothers. Glad y'all could make it. If you would, let's quit passing that jug now and get this meeting started. Anybody got any old business? No? Well, let's open the floor for new business. Brother Earl, what's on your mind?"

"I'd like to thank the honorable Great Gator for recogniz—"

"'Scuse me, Brother Earl, but that's Grand Dragon. I'm the Grand Dragon. I know you're new in the Klan, boy, but it's high time you got your reptiles straight."

"Sorry, Mister, uh, Dragon. Anyway, I think some of y'all knew Edna and me been having trouble making suits for the young'uns that really fit good. But just last week, Edna wised up and figured out how to make little bitty Klan suits out of pillowcases. They look real nice. And she wanted y'all to know that the Martha Stewart pillowcase collection is on sale. Including the extra large size."

"That's fine, brother. I'm sure we'll remember that. Now, I've got some bad news. I know y'all been excited 'cause Halloween's coming and we thought we'd finally get a chance to put on our robes and masks and march without being hassled. Turns out we can't. Leastwise, not with our masks on. The law says long as we're in our Klan suits, no masks allowed. And I know we ain't much for that these days. Which means I guess there won't be any of us out there Trick or Treating for God and country this year. Sorry, fellas.

"So, this meeting's adjourned. We'll head on out to the cross burning now. Brother Ed has a couple of paint-stirring sticks he's gonna torch up tonight. Wish we could still burn them big ones like we used to, but lumber and kerosene's way up and membership's down and we just can't afford it no more."

There's trouble between the sheets in Klan country. You can thank the Georgia General Assembly.

For years the Ku Klux Klan was free to play Trick or Treat whenever they liked, donning their white robes and pointy hoods and heading out to wreak mischief and misery on anybody who didn't look, think or act like them. They were so proud of their work they hid behind masks.

The Georgia General Assembly finally got fed up with these shenanigans and passed a law making it illegal to wear a hood or a mask or any device that conceals a person's identity. They did, however, exempt Halloween costumes.

It was a loophole the loonies leaped at. This year two Klan groups got all fired up and planned Halloween day marches in Gainesville, Georgia, hoping to take advantage of the Halloween mask exemption. They believed the Klan outfit qualified as a Halloween costume, making it within the law.

Unfortunately for the Klan, Hall County Sheriff Bob Vass had another opinion. He expressed it last week, telling the Klan, "If they've got on a Klan robe and a Klan hat and any type of mask, including a Mickey Mouse mask, they will be arrested."

So far, none of the Klanspersons appears willing to risk jail over this alleged First Amendment oppression. And it seems that the decision to march was based not so much on conviction as convenience. Gary Mallincoat, spokesman for one of the Klan groups, says the Klan's action was contemplated "...because we thought we could get away with it."

For shame, fellas. Where are your principles? And why the masks, anyway? If you guys are so proud of yourselves, you should be eager to show your smiling faces as you proclaim who you are and what you stand for.

Of course, maybe the marches weren't really canceled for lack of courage. There could be a health risk involved. I understand some lizards just can't stand the light of day.

Bothersome Barbecue

This is a tale of clashing cultures. One of those incidents that was bound to happen as unfamiliar elbows begin to rub in the ever-shrinking global village we all call home.

It was a balmy spring Saturday in Suwanee, Georgia. The sun was bright, the birds were chirping and Cathi Herrera and her husband, Angel, decided to fire up the backyard grill. A few drinks, a nice piece of meat, what could be better. The grocery shopping went off without a hitch. The cooking was another story entirely.

All the Herreras wanted was a taste of home. A little barbecue, just like they enjoyed back in Mexico. And there should have been no problem. After all, barbecue's barbecue, right?

Well, yes and no. You see, the Herreras wanted to grill a goat. They went to the local meat-packing house and selected a low-mileage, tender young beast sporting fleshy flanks and juicy ribs. They threw the creature in the back of the car and headed home, dreaming of a dinner worthy of a full spread in *Gourmet* magazine. There was only one small glitch in the plan, a decidedly non-Martha Stewart touch... the Herreras' entree was still breathing.

When they returned home, the evening meal was released into the backyard, where it frolicked with the Herrera kids while Angel put some mariachi music on the boom box and set fire to a mound of charcoal.

Next-door neighbor Susan Pike, tanning on her deck, observed the scene with a smile. She was delighted when she saw the Herreras' children playing with the goat, thinking it was a pet. Her smile faded, however, when the animal began to bleat with alarm as the elder Herrera grabbed it by its feet, turned it upside down and began sharpening all manner of tools in preparation for slaughtering the animal. Ms. Pike, you see, is a supporter of animal rights. She also frowns on eating red meat, not to mention dispatching it on the hoof. Especially next door.

Believing the Herreras' style of food preparation was a bit too Old Testament for upscale Suwanee, Pike fought back a rowdy gag reflex and swung into action to save the beast from becoming a feast.

She first called her friend Linda Brotherton, who lives on the other side of the Herreras and is also a vegetarian and animal activist. Brotherton called the law while Pike headed to the Herreras' yard to plead for a stay of execution.

Luckily, authorities arrived while the goat was still intact. After a heated discussion, the barbecue was called off, and Pike and Brotherton produced a friend who purchased the goat from the Herreras and took it away to greener, and less terminal, pastures. The Herreras used the proceeds from the sale of the goat to buy some burgers, which they grilled in a nearby park.

Still steamed after the incident, neighbor Brotherton said, "I don't think the fact that it's for food consumption justifies it." Neighbor Pike agreed, adding, "I don't care what people eat. You just don't slaughter it in your backyard."

Or do you? Suwanee Police Chief Mike Boyd said that his office had recently been called about a man who was slaughtering a deer in his yard.

184

Angel Herrera saw nothing wrong with his actions, saying that in Mexico, slaughtering a goat was no different than killing a deer and eating it.

Cathi Herrera was stunned by the whole affair. She said, "I didn't do it to offend them (the neighbors). I did it because I wanted some goat. If I could find dead goat at Kroger, I'd buy it."

Patience, Ms. Herrera. As the waters of cultural diversity rise ever higher around these parts, I have a feeling it won't be long before you get your wish.

THE HUMAN
CONDITION

I spend half my time wondering, "How can people do this
to each other?" and the other half hoping
I'm not doing the same thing without knowing it.

The Price of Innocence

Her front license plate said "Jesus Is The Reason." I don't think it referred to the bashed-in driver's side door and mangled front quarter panel.

It was a few weeks back, a picture-book Sunday morning. Dogwoods sagged with fat blooms under an aquarium-clear sky, and a taste of wind churned the pollen and hustled the grass clippings down the gutter.

Sunday School done and early church obviously attended, she was walking away from the big sanctuary, heading for the battered Ford in front of the pizza joint.

Her look was distant, anxious. Around her, two young boys darted in and out, circling like puppies on an invisible leash. Their matching khaki pants were creased sharp, shirts unwrinkled, sneakers off-brand but clean and scuff-free. They were a study in well-cared-for.

She wasn't, quite. Her tan gabardine Sunday suit was limp and shiny from endless encounters with washer and iron. The high-necked white blouse was dingy at the collar and frayed at the cuff. Worn, short-heeled black pumps clattered on the concrete, keeping time to the chorus of "Watch outs" and "Come backs" issued to the kids.

In her right hand she clutched a Bible like a lover to her breast. With her left she pried the car door open with a loud metallic protest. Over the noise, the boys were asking, "When is Daddy coming? He's taking us to McDonald's."

Without answering, she loaded them up and drove off, the dinged-up vehicle listing slightly to port and coughing fog from the muffler.

I don't know the woman. I can guess the story.

Divorced, struggling, a refugee from those private wars where gold bands of eternal love are melted down to 14 karat ammunition. Raising her kids mostly alone, counting pennies for lunch money, hoping the shoes last until summer.

Trying to do the right thing. Seeing that the two boys had what they needed. Not Rollerblades or GI Joes or Beanie Babies but things more precious: love and attention and care. It was clear she had chosen to do the best by her boys even if it meant doing without for herself.

A few weeks later, a few miles north, another woman made a different choice. If news stories are correct, she "sold" her three- and four-year-old nieces to a man who sexually molested them. She used the money to buy drugs, trading seven years of innocence for two rocks of crack.

Tells you a lot about the society we live in. About what matters to people and what doesn't. To one woman, it was taking care of her children at any cost. To another, it was taking care of herself, and the children be damned.

Two women, four children. Forty miles and light years apart. They made their choices. They'll get their rewards.

One already has, a half-hour thrill ride on a cocaine carousel. I hope she remembers it to her dying day, which, if there's any justice in the world, will be soon.

The other won't get her reward for a few more years, when those two boys think back, remember her sacrifice, and thank her for it.

Of course those two little girls will have childhood memories, too. But not of bright, breezy Sundays at church. They'll have the other kind. The kind that years of psychiatric soap can't wash away.

I hate to say it, but I hope those two little girls never get washed up and shined up and dolled up on the Lord's Day. Hope they never go to church or Sunday School. If they do, they may learn something ugly. That they not only got sold out, but sold too cheap.

You see, they only fetched fifteen bucks.

I'm afraid if they read the Bible they may learn that for the kind of betrayal they suffered, thirty pieces of silver is the traditional fee.

Managing Memories a Little Better

The preacher should have charged double. But at the time he didn't realize he was burying two people in the small metal coffin.

The police report said the kid never saw it coming. He was so carried away with his new Christmas bicycle he just shot down the little slope in the cemetery and raced across the street to the driveway where his mother, father and twin brother stood waiting. His brother remembered he even let out a whoop of delight as he bumped over the curb and into the path of the truck that killed him.

I missed the funeral, but everyone said it was nice, with pleasant words about the young boy's life and appropriate remarks about him being "taken before his time" and the usual reminders that such things are "part of a larger plan" and "meant to be."

The family was well liked in the little town, and everyone turned out, from the doctors and dentists and bankers who served as local royalty right down to the mill workers and peanut farmers.

After the last "Amen," the father and mother and brother went home, intending to pick up the pieces and put their lives back together. It didn't quite work out.

I moved away a few months after the accident and got the story in installments from friends over the coming years. And the story wasn't all good.

I understand the surviving twin son grew up well-adjusted and seemingly happy. He left the town as soon as he graduated from high school and rarely came home, never at Christmas.

The father was a plumber and a member of the little country club with the nine-hole golf course and the small, cozy, dark-paneled bar. He still found his way to the regular Wednesday afternoon and Saturday morning golf gatherings, but in time his clubs gathered dust as he gave up golf altogether and spent his country club time hunched over the bar.

In a few years his business failed, followed shortly afterwards by his liver, pickled by too much booze. He was buried next to his child. Folks said he didn't drink so much to grieve the loss of his son but the loss of his wife.

Everyone agreed the mother took it hardest. She wasn't a drinker, so she decided to drown herself in grief. Especially at Christmas.

When friends tried to help or suggest she get on with life, she wouldn't hear of it. She wielded her grief like a club, screaming, "You don't know what it's like to lose a child. You can never be happy after that."

And to prove it, she never was.

It turned out bad all right, but it didn't have to. When she sorted through her memories, she couldn't see the bright ones any more...they floated away like silvery bubbles, leaving her to ponder only cold lumps of despair. I hear the days around Christmas were the worst of all.

I don't think it had to happen that way. I know another woman in another town who also lost a young child under tragic circumstances, but she didn't let it end her life.

This woman grieved and she missed her child, too, but when she remembered him, she remembered the good things. She remembered her boy's smile, and it put one on her face. She remembered his laugh, and it made her chuckle, too. She remembered the joy he had brought her, not the pain of his loss. She treated her memories like family silver, kept them polished and shiny and precious. Her Christmases continued to be good ones.

The "experts" say the Christmas season can be especially rough on people. Perhaps, but maybe things could improve if folks just managed their memories better. We all have bad ones, but we all have good ones, too.

And we'd all do well to remember that while memories have the power to cripple, they also have the power to heal.

Health Nuts

Falling school test scores, rising crime rates, environmental damage, terrorism. Everybody worries about something these days.

For me, it's vacations. And the fact that Americans seem to have forgotten how to take them. When I was a kid, a vacation was something the whole family looked forward to. Especially a trip to the beach. It was a time to let your hair down, wear your rattiest clothes, sleep late—or not at all—and spend as much time as you could doing absolutely nothing you didn't absolutely love.

When people get away these days, nothing changes but the zip code. The last time I went to the beach I did my best to keep the tradition alive. I didn't shave, barely bathed, wore my worst clothes. But I was surrounded by folks looking and doing exactly as they do back wherever they came from.

Same designer clothes. Same immaculate makeup, and worst of all, same nasty exercise habits.

A walk on the beach is one thing, but these days the beach towns are covered with joggers. It's supposed to be vacation. Why make it torture? And don't tell me it isn't. Joggers may say, "I just love it," but their faces tell a different story. When's the last time you saw a jogger smile? Never. Unless they're on that last hundred-foot burst to the margarita machine.

This whole thing is just wrong.

As proof I go back to the Bible. Adam and Eve each came with a set of legs, not a pair of Air Jordans. And they used those legs to walk out of the Garden of Eden. Moses walked out of Egypt to the Promised Land. And while Jesus may have taken a boat ride or two when he hung out with the fishermen, he didn't jog into Jerusalem on Palm Sunday. For high-speed travel, he used a donkey.

Where in the world did we get the idea that jogging is a good thing?

The first recorded jog is in a Greek tale about some dude who ran 26 miles to Athens from a place called Marathon to announce the Greeks had won a battle. Then he promptly fell over dead. That should have been a clue.

To be fair, maybe I'm just showing my age. And my upbringing. When I grew up, nobody jogged. As far as I know, nobody even thought about it. Mothers stayed home and kept house. For exercise, they chased unruly children. Fathers toiled all day, and when they got home, the last thing they wanted was another workout. If dad had a little extra stress, he didn't jog it off. He stopped for a beer on the way home.

In high school no one—other than athletes—ran. I can't recall a soul who ran for "fun." In college the only volunteer runners I saw were members of the track team and Hare Krishna trainees learning how to escape a lynch mob.

Jogging is now a national mania. Or maybe obsession is the better word, for it appears fitness nuts are so dedicated they won't let anything come between them and their workout. Not even death.

I learned this from a wire report datelined Englewood, Colorado. It concerned a man who fell over dead of a heart attack. While he was working out. In a health club.

Paramedics were summoned, and here's where it gets really good. The whole time paramedics worked on the heart attack victim, not a soul stopped working out.

But wait—there's more. Paramedics finally declared the guy dead and turned him over to health club officials...who called the funeral home.

Then they covered the deceased with a sheet and left the man exactly where he had dropped dead.

The hearse didn't arrive for two hours.

And the whole time the dead man lay there, guess what? Everyone went about their business as usual. Spinners kept spinning, lifters kept lifting, joggers kept jogging...and not a single soul complained about the corpse.

That's healthy?

A Man Worth Admiring

Harold Toomer had worked at the cotton mill in south Alabama since the day he quit junior high. He was a bear of a man, tall and barrel-chested, but quiet until things got tense. He wore blue coveralls to work every day, lived in a shotgun house in the mill village, and as long as I knew him never drove a new car or wore anything other than steel-toed work boots.

He said "oncet" for once and "twicet" for twice and his grammar was garbled as Sanskrit. He was one of the finest men I ever knew.

I met Harold on a Tuesday night. I was teaching music, and it was the fall of the year, the time when school band directors made recruiting pitches to the fifth graders. I went around banging rhythm sticks and playing recorders, trying to drum up a few more bodies to fill the closet full of uniforms left over after graduation, boredom and the lure of the more socially acceptable football had taken its toll on the musical ranks.

The man from the music store was there, his van full of shiny new horns, brass and silver offerings designed to dazzle and tempt young minds. He let students blat a trombone, buzz a trumpet, honk the saxophone, and attempt to make a flute do something other than go "Whifff."

At his urgings, and mine, recommendations were made to the kids, based on first, their aptitude for a particular horn, and second, the director's immediate needs.

In other words, if the trombone section was looking thin for the next year or so, it was amazing how many kids were suddenly long-armed enough to pump that slide.

We had a good crowd that night, and one of the last to try out was a beautiful little blond girl, with clear blue eyes, a sweet smile and Harold Toomer for a daddy.

She tried her hand at several instruments and finally chose, without any urging, the clarinet.

The way the system worked, once an instrument was selected, the music salesman offered the parents several buying options. The most popular plan was a down payment and monthlies thereafter, a cautious way to pay for a potential whim.

When Sherry Toomer walked up, the music store man reached over and handed her a clarinet, a wood one, good quality, shiny and clean and new.

Then he looked at her father, standing there in his clean but worn coveralls, on his way to the third shift. In his slow, deep voice, he spoke only two words: "How much?"

As the music man began to explain the payment plan, Harold interrupted and said, "I'll pay for it now."

With that, he reached into his pocket, pulled out three hundred dollars in crumpled twenties, fives and tens and handed them over, then waited for his receipt.

The music man, sensing the financial sacrifice being made, tried to hand the money back, gently advising that the installment plan would be easier on the wallet. Harold just shook his head, saying, "If she wants it and she'll stick with it, she's gonna have it. And it ain't hers till it's paid for. Now it's hers."

For the next four years of our acquaintance, when band activities required parental help, Harold was always the first to volunteer, the first to get there and the last to leave, doing whatever chore he was assigned with pride and quiet dignity. His kids went to college and grew up just as fine as you'd expect.

He was just a decent, honest man who never made a headline or hit a hole-in-one. Never did anything much except to love his wife, do his job and raise his kids right. He said himself he was nothing special.

Wonder why I can't forget him?

Dontory Jordan Lived and Died the Same Way...Hungry

He was a small kid to begin with, weighing only five pounds, eleven ounces at birth. Small, but he must have been a scrapper, because the day he went for his two-month doctor's appointment, he was still alive. That's quite a feat, considering his weight by then had dropped to three pounds, seven ounces.

The doctors were shocked. In his eight weeks on earth, the infant boy had lost almost half his body weight.

Dontory's problem was a birth defect. Its name is Diana Meeks. On his birth certificate, she's listed as his mother. On the police report, she's named as his killer.

But there are two sides to every story. If asked, I'm sure Diana would say she was doing her best to be a good mother.

After all, she did take little Dontory to his two-month medical check-up. That's where his doctors became alarmed at his emaciated state. So alarmed, in fact, that rather than waste precious minutes waiting for an ambulance, the doctors instructed Diana to get in her car and take Dontory immediately to the hospital for emergency care.

Diana flew from the office, Dontory cradled in her arms. The hospital was only minutes away. It would be all right. The child would be saved.

But he wasn't. Rather than race towards help, Diana made a stop. And looking back, I guess you really can't blame her. After all, she was taking her baby to the hospital and hospitals are packed with patients and doctors and nurses and visitors. Everyone wants to look their best in that situation.

Dontory's mother was no exception. She just wanted to look her best. Surely that's it. Surely that's why she interrupted a life-or-death race to the hospital to pull over and have her nails done.

Diana took Dontory into the nail salon, and while her cuticles were being massaged, he lay quietly beside her, wrapped in a blanket.

That's where he died. Right there on the floor of the nail parlor on the way to the hospital. That's where he died of starvation.

Apparently, he'd been dying for a while. The autopsy revealed that at the time of his death, not a trace of food was present in Dontory's body. Not a trace.

His mother had simply starved him to death. Obviously it wasn't for lack of money. With cash for nails and cars, there was surely some for a meal now and then.

People involved with the case are at a loss to explain the mother's behavior, including the mother herself, who has yet to speak publicly about her actions. Maybe she's still trying to puzzle things out.

I wish I could say she'll have a lifetime in jail to think it over, but she won't. After starving her child to death, after performing a deed as coldly premeditated as any murder, Diana Meeks was found guilty only of involuntary manslaughter. She'll spend four years in jail, perhaps less, with time off for good behavior.

So Heaven gets a new tenant way too early and a mother with a high-priced manicure will spend a few years watching free cable and enjoying something she never provided her own son...three meals a day. Welcome to justice, nineties-style.

And while every life is precious, considering what he might have endured being raised by a soul-scarred piece of human garbage like Diana Meeks, this baby is surely better off with the angels.

Here on earth, Dontory Jordan must have had a last supper. Unfortunately, no one knows when it was. At least now, he won't have to worry about missing any more meals.

I hear the food's pretty good in Heaven. I hope the little guy gets all he wants.

Patches

The voice on the other end of the line promised an interesting story. We met and I listened. Turned out it was nothing new as human relationships go, but still, it left me thinking. And for some reason, remembering the jeans I wore when I was a kid.

Vivid indigo and store-creased when new, they chafed and scratched, brittle and raspy. They were tough at first, but in time they changed. I watched it happen from my window in the back of the house.

The view was plain. A pasture where eventually houses would grow instead of hay. A pecan tree too young to bear fruit but large enough to shade a small patio. And the clothesline, a set of scaly, steel posts crossed by two wooden planks joined by four lengths of stiff dark wire. Over the years I saw it play host to underwear, T-shirts, the occasional mockingbird or squirrel, and of course, the blue jeans.

At day's end the jeans were filled with sweat, blood, dirt, grass, hurt and every other concoction a young kid could dabble in. But just one trip through the washer and they emerged clean and bright, ready for another day, another dose of boy.

All year I watched them. Turning slowly in a cool autumn breeze, hanging limp in the August heat. On gray-curtained winter days and bright spring mornings and ice-white summer days they hung there like condemned men, clipped with wooden pins to a backyard gallows.

New, they were brazen and rough, angry, flushed with color. But as the days and weeks passed, those brittle, starchy jeans began to soften, to let go of their stiff pride.

By Christmas the back-to-school pair were soft as a first-date kiss. Summer found the Christmas offerings thin and light, bright blue banners faded to limp, pale rags.

And with the fading came the markings of time. A pull here, a thinning, a rip that threatened to become a tear. Signs of wear. Signs of living.

My mother didn't think twice when the first rip appeared. Out came the needle and out came the patches and with a stitch or two, the jeans were ready for another wearing.

Those patches were an amazement. As if forged from a magic loom, they were strong as denim steel, ungiving, unflinching, tough.

In time the jeans wore thin, the patches never. And with each new rip, another patch was applied until some of those jeans appeared like leopards from a Technicolor fantasy, pale blue creatures spotted with dark violet.

Life's a lot like those worn jeans. Events cause rips and tears and breaks; things get frayed and worn and pulled apart. When that happens, you have a choice: to either throw things away and say forget it or take up a needle and patch the problem. Sew it tight and strong.

And then send things back to the laundry room to soak out the troubles of the day. After each washing, you'll generally find that not only are the stains mostly gone, but something else has happened. Things may be a bit more fragile, but at the same time a bit more familiar, a bit more like home.

Years ago I got in the habit of buying new when the rips started to show. It was just easier. But lately I think it might be best if more of us got the needle out again and did some patching.

Chances are we'll not only get a little more mileage out of what appears to be a worn-out situation but discover something new as well.

That a patched-up life may not look as good as a shiny new one, but in most cases, like those old, faded, worn-out jeans, the lives with all the patches are not only the most comfortable...

They're the strongest, too.

Not-So-Little Girl Lost

Six or so hours after the last cork had popped "hello" to 1998, she was on the street a few blocks from the court square, sipping coffee from a paper cup and looking to sell her body for a few bucks or a bottle of beer. Brand-new year, same old girl.

I met her over a year ago when she approached me for a ride home and offered sex in return. She got the ride, I passed on the payment.

Since then, she's come by the office a time or two. I've bought her a couple of Big Macs and she's told me bits and pieces of her story. I wanted to write it once, but the urge has passed.

And there she was on New Year's Day. Alone, walking in the barely bright morning, wrapped in heavy coat, leggings and scarf, looking for a handout to get through another day.

I thought once that hers would be an interesting tale, the story of a garden-variety streetwalker who chose not to ply her trade at a big-city intersection but along the gentle lanes of small-town America.

The story of a woman so addicted to crack and alcohol she would live anywhere, do anything, to get another jolt, not too proud to ask a stranger for money, to swap sex for cash, to stuff a steaming free burger between her cheeks while begging for a five spot.

She had a good job once, and a good man, she says. They repaired computers, or maybe TVs. The story changes. Her husband died young and she moved to Newnan seven years ago to stay with friends. She has two children who live here with "grandparents," or maybe friends. That part changes, too.

I asked where she was living these days. With another "boyfriend," she said brightly, one who didn't hit her like the others. What a gift, I thought, to find happiness in a blow unstruck.

We talked briefly, and I had to go, as did she. She asked for a handout, offering again that oldest of collaterals as security.

I passed. I'd offered assistance before, offered to help get her cleaned up and straightened out. She wasn't interested. Now, neither was I.

I offered to buy her a biscuit stuffed with eggs and ham, but she said no, that she'd rather have the cash to shop for herself. From her breath, still reeking of alcohol, I knew what size brown bag she'd leave the store with.

And so I drove off, leaving her silhouetted in the just-rising sun, breath coming in ragged, frosty patches from her lipstick-smeared mouth.

I don't worry about her anymore. She's a survivor, not by accident, but choice. Such a pitiful ambition for someone who lives in a land so thick with opportunities you have to dodge them to walk down the street.

And I've had enough. No longer will I feel pity for her. She has chosen her path, and as far as I'm concerned, she can walk it alone.

She said she once had it good, yet now she's content to exist at the meanest level we can conceive, willing to part with any shred of dignity or slip of flesh for a few hours with a bottle or a few minutes with a crack pipe.

Is the dope that good? The booze? Or has her life become so hopeless that she nurses her addiction as a way just to survive?

Somehow, I think neither. I think she's just chosen the easy way out.

After all, it's easier to spend five minutes on your back with a stranger than to punch a clock for eight hours day after day. It's easier to drive through a fog of dope with your life on low beams than to pay the bills or raise the kids.

Yeah, it's easier. Some people just prefer it that way, and sadly, she's one of them.

Choices

She never mentioned it and neither did I, and after a week, maybe ten days, the bruise on her left eye was hardly noticeable, no more than a pale blue necklace circling the space between her cheekbone and brow.

She wore it every day on that eleven-to-seven shift, taking money and making change, never offering an explanation to the questions her customers left unasked.

Her children showed up every morning toward the end of her shift, driven into town by their grandparents, who had obviously been pressed into duty to help raise the child of the child they'd raised. Around six or so every morning, they'd drop the little ones off and visit with their daughter, giving details on the kids' activities and asking quietly about recent run-ins with the husband.

After saying hello, the kids would immediately head for the candy display, only to be told time and again, "No," that the lunch money would stay in their pockets until they left for school.

The little girl mostly kept quiet, stood by her grandmother and stared at the strangers dropping in for predawn coffee and snacks. The little boy was quite vocal about school. He didn't like it, never wanted to go, said he hated the classwork and the teachers. More than once he asked his mother if his daddy had been making trouble again.

It didn't take a genius to figure out the situation. It was discussed right there in the open in front of perfect strangers and the beer salesman. Guess if the pain gets bad enough, you don't care who hears you cry out.

I wondered what a woman with a black eye and two scared kids asks God for every night when she hits her knees.

I wondered what she would have thought about another woman I saw recently. She was on a Home and Garden TV special babbling on about "the hardest decision I ever had to make in my life." She was talking about choosing paint colors for her new multimillion-dollar mansion.

Funny how our disasters differ. For one woman the problem was trying to keep her job and protect her kids from an abusive father. For the other it was having a zillion-dollar budget at Sherwin-Williams and not being able to pull the trigger between ice blue and robin's egg.

No judging here, I just find it amusing that we live in a country where people can prosper to the point where choosing between paint colors is a serious chore. And the woman on TV isn't the only one tortured by such minor aggravations.

I know another woman whose husband promised her a new car of her choice for Christmas. She pestered her friends endlessly about whether to choose a Mercedes or a Volvo.

I know another couple who practically came to blows over what wine to serve with dinner. It was that important. To them, it was life or death. It mattered. They cared.

And that's fine. We should care about things, even the little things. But when we treat everything as a crisis then nothing is truly important. And that cheapens the value of the really tough decisions, which sooner or later, we all have to make.

Nothing against the folks who have a hard time picking wallpaper, but if they really want to make a tough call, they should try choosing between shoes and food.

No Way to Teach a Lesson

Like the song says, "Some days are diamonds, some days are stones."
Stick this one in the non-precious category.

Oh, the day's all right, I guess. It's the news that's bad.

I don't know why this particular story hit me so hard. After all, in the past few months I've read about prom queens leaving newborns in the restroom to die and a mother whose two children baked to death in her car while she played air-conditioned video poker and about some guy in New York giving AIDS to a group of teenage girls, and a 13-year-old killer who shot a man dead for not dimming his headlights.

Still, this one got to me. Maybe because it happened in Iowa, where I thought people still lived normal lives and put hands over hearts for the National Anthem. Guess I was wrong, because two of the state's finest young corn-fed lads, Chad Lamansky and Daniel Myers, were just found guilty of a crime that makes me want to throw up.

They were convicted of murdering 16 victims and wounding seven others. They did it with baseball bats.

The victims were all cats. These punks broke into the Noah's Ark animal sanctuary and did their damage on a whim, stroking their victims into eternity like so many fur-covered hanging curve balls.

Here's the best part. The kids were found guilty of misdemeanor, not felony, charges. And not because the crimes weren't heartless or atrocious or disgusting.

No, they faced the reduced charges because a jury ruled that the cats weren't worth a collective 500 bucks. Under Iowa law, if the cats had been valued at over $500, the killers would have faced felony charges punishable by 10 years in jail and $15,000 in fines.

Now, the most they'll get is five years and a $750 slap on the wrist. Nobody expects them to do any jail time.

I wish I could think of some way to make these kids pay a higher price for this vicious act. If not, what lesson will their punishment teach them?

That if you're going to torture and kill something, make sure it's not worth much?

What a courtroom spectacle. Two sets of lawyers arguing about whether a cat's worth more than $31.50 a pop for batting practice. Here's my question: when did judicial punishment become based on the dollar value of the victim?

Ask any owner, "What's your dog worth? Your cat?" They can't tell you. You can't measure loyalty and friendship with a dollar sign. You measure a pet's worth in the joy it gives you, and the love. Far as I know, they haven't fixed a price for those qualities yet. But as I said, that's not the bad part. Just the fact that two kids in Iowa decided to spend their Friday night battering 16 defenseless animals to death tells me we have worse problems in this country than I thought.

The state argued that the cats were indeed worth 32 bucks because of the shelter's cost to acquire them. The defense said the shelter got strays for free and that the prosecution's contention that local pet stores get thirty bucks for a kitten wouldn't wash, because "it was apples and oranges."

"Those were kittens," they said. "People don't want old, stray adult cats."

Well, finally. When you put it that way, it makes sense. Old cats aren't as much fun as kittens. Old cats just hang around and sleep and annoy you. And occasionally, love you.

Yep, older critters are a little more trouble. And who needs the aggravation? When it comes to old ones, the fewer the better.

Bet that's something these kids' parents will think about next time the little darlings grab a bat off the rack.

Finding Hope on the Side of the Road

Christmas is a tough season, one we fight with, struggle against. A time we hoard our evergreens to brighten the dismal bedclothes Mother Nature wears during her annual nap. A time we hang colored lights from trees and homes to lengthen the shortened, gray days. A time we play cheerful music to warm frosted hearts.

It's a time that can get you down. It had me on the ropes not long ago.

A day-long Saturday storm had left the Sunday morning streets littered with leaves. They lay in the street like small, sodden flyers declaring winter officially open for business.

I took a drive, hoping to clear my head and maybe find a sliver of sunshine hiding behind the gray overcast.

On a favorite back road, a rambling two-lane south of town, I noticed a small cross on the side of the road. They're not that uncommon anymore, usually marking the site where an accident victim perished, but this one caught my eye because of its size.

The cross was tiny, maybe eight inches high, made from a couple of those thin sticks used to stir paint. It was painted white and rested at one end of a small mound of dirt.

Scrawled on the crosspiece in a child's hand were two words, "My Puppy."

It sat at the mouth of a long gravel driveway leading to a modest green frame house. In the front yard were a swing set and a plastic three-wheeler, pink and white, with plastic streamers hung from the handlebars.

Sitting there, I wondered if the driver of that small vehicle had been the one who had lettered the simple marker, helped dig the small grave and lay to rest a four-legged beast that died too young to even have a name. Was the child who fashioned the crude marker a boy or a girl? And how old, five, six, maybe eight?

Of course, those questions didn't really matter. What did matter was that whoever had performed this small act of love was aware that even the most humble of creatures deserves at least a mention.

The puppy in the hole had obviously made an impact on someone. Enough that they chose to mark its absence for all to see. To say to the passing world, "Here lies something that was precious to me. Take notice."

It occurred to me that in that small green house, a child had learned some important lessons about caring and love and respect.

In the week since, the news has been filled with stories about other children who obviously hadn't been taught so well; reports of teenagers leaving newborns to die in trash cans, committing assaults, rapes, murders, even shooting a school prayer group full of holes shortly after the morning's last amen.

I wonder if the kids involved in those hideous crimes had ever buried a puppy, had ever learned the value of caring about a pet, much less a parent or a peer.

Sometimes it seems like we've raised a whole generation of kids so starved for values and morals that they have no concept of what's even proper, much less right or wrong.

I know all kids aren't that way, it's just that the rotten apples get all the ink. And I don't believe the bad ones are born that way. With rare exceptions, kids learn to become what they are. Usually from parents. Some learn to become bad. Some learn to become good—like the kid who made the little cross.

For me, that small grave was a comfort. A simple statement that something, anything, still counts. I left the place wearing my first smile of the day.

As long as there are still kids around with enough heart to bury a puppy, maybe there's still hope for us all.

Unhappy Endings

She speaks, he listens, they split.

And as their dream crumbled, the earth spun on, missed not one beat, unmoved by their personal earthquake. In the end, they were simply a set of mismatched heartbeats.

I've known this couple for a while, and watched them with interest, and some concern, as things played out. We wouldn't qualify as best friends, but I feel I know them well enough to write this requiem for a relationship.

In the beginning they shared a happy lunacy, with just the right balance of heat and light, the proper mix of laughter and concern. In the beginning their hopes soared on the wings of expectation. In the beginning they were certain their past mistakes could be overcome.

In the end they couldn't. They were victims of the fairy tale...the one that promises the brass ring to be an easier catch on the second spin. For them it wasn't. They felt their situation was unique, but in truth it was not. The tale has been told often. Only the characters change, often unaware that they're following a script as old as time.

In the end, they were confused, shaken, wondering how it could have gone so wrong. They had made all the right plans, had all the right discussions, read all the right books.

They had good intentions, but needed more. In times of stress, their problems drove them apart rather than together. They lacked that magical glue that binds two people so tightly they can stand against any odds. Their supply of trust was too small for the journey they planned.

The first signs of trouble went unnoticed, the last screamed like neon billboards...

The perceived verbal slight became a reason not to speak at all. The hands that once sparked at the slightest touch no longer reached for each other. The gentle, once-welcomed touches were somehow seen as assaults, misplaced, misunderstood, misguided.

The long, talking walks were reduced to a series of silent, fitful footsteps from room to room. Their friends speculated on the demise. Not enough tears, they said, or perhaps too many. Or perhaps it was a case of too much talk and not enough listen. Or perhaps it was something else entirely.

Some relationships are juicy and fat, running red with blood and passion, ripped with tissue, tight and strong. Theirs seemed thin, fragile, susceptible to the first high wind or shudder underfoot.

When they sensed trouble, they looked desperately for help, for a solution, for a thread of hope to stitch their remaining pieces of happiness back together.

They tried, but the promises they piled so high were thin as meringue, subject to toppling by the slightest breeze.

In all likelihood, theirs was simply a rhythm problem. Marriage was a dance they had learned with other partners, and after years in the stag line, they found they'd forgotten the steps.

Their together died of a neglect nourished by bitter memories that neither could erase. Memories that left him unable to take his heart off the leash, her unable to commit to someone she had not conceived. Neither was to blame. They are good people and they tried, tried hard. Sometimes, these things are not meant to be.

They played a game of romantic chicken and everyone lost. It ended calmly, with no bitter tears or curses, but rather with a moan, a snuffle, an open-eyed astonishment at what had occurred. The last entry in their emotional inventory was a shared question as to what went wrong.

She speaks, he listens, they split. And so it ends. Not with a bang, or even a whimper, but with stillness. And silence. A loud, long silence.

ME AND THE CATS

I started to call this section "Jesus Didn't Have a Cat."

I know that's true because cats are not mentioned in the Bible.

If Jesus had owned one, we'd have heard about it.

Losing the Magic Touch

They say it's like riding a bicycle.

They say once you've done it you never forget how.

They say it's a piece of cake.

They lie.

A few weeks ago, my ex-cat George moved back in with me while he recovered from major (for a cat) surgery on what passes (in cat anatomy) for a knee. I figured taking care of him would be a snap. After all, I tended him through his early shots and wormings and soothed his first scrapes and scratches.

I even nurtured him through his neutering. It wasn't as bad as I thought, since it gave us something in common to talk about while we watched SportsCenter on ESPN.

But that was then. This is now. It's been a few years since I was his sole caregiver, and my cat-care skills have obviously eroded.

When I brought him home from the hospital, the routine was fairly simple. Since his left leg was encased in a splint-like contraption that started below his toes and extended above his hip, he was basically immobile. All he could do was lie on the floor and flop from side to side, much like a beached carp. My job mostly consisted of rubbing his belly, singing an occasional favorite from *Cats* and sticking his food and water dish under his nose.

That first night, since he was in a new place and feeling miserable, I put him on the bed with me, hoping it would comfort him. After he flopped off the bed twice in less than an hour, I left him on the floor with a dirty T-shirt he seemed fond of. The next day the drugs wore off and his digestive system came back to life and we figured out how to use the litter box. Together. This is not something I recommend.

He eventually learned to hobble around with the splinted limb stuck out beside him like an outrigger on a Hawaiian canoe. The outrigger was a problem. I wound up going home several times each day to make sure he hadn't gotten tangled up in something. Once he got jammed in the TV cabinet. Another time, he managed to wedge the splint under the bed, which I had to take apart to set him free.

We both rejoiced when the splint was replaced by a cast. George because it gave him better mobility, me because he could use the litter box by himself.

The physical recovery is going nicely. But now there's another problem.

I'd forgotten how quickly cats learn your routine and adapt it to their own, mostly selfish needs. And I'd forgotten that upon arising, George's most desperate need is food to keep his none-too-slender 23-pound frame from withering to normal proportions.

Work requires me to rise early each day, and therefore, I treasure every precious second of sleep. George is less concerned with my sleep than his belly. He knows he'll get fed at 3:30, but sometimes, he can't (or won't) wait. Some days I'm awakened at 2:00 or 2:30 or 3:17 by a fat, fuzzy paw slapping me softly in the face. Or, if I don't jump right up, slapping me not so softly. In a pinch, he'll resort to walking on my head.

I tried throwing a handful of food into the next room and sticking my head under the covers, hoping he'd forget me. Didn't work. I tried shutting him in the next room at bedtime. He whined so loudly I couldn't get to sleep.

I finally did the sensible thing and gave up. Now, I set the clock, hope for the best and expect the worst. My dream is that when he's fully recovered, his sleep cycle will match mine and we'll all be dozing happily through the night.

Of course, there could be even worse problems ahead. Now that he's feeling better, George says he's lonely. I think he wants his sister Tammy to move in.

All of a sudden, I'm the one who's starting to feel sick.

The Horror Begins, Again

Once upon a time, fall was my favorite season. World Series, football, beautiful scenery, cool weather, fall had it all. Or used to. This year, I'm not looking forward to it. Last year changed my autumn outlook for good.

Not surprisingly, a female was involved.

Sooner or later every relationship reaches a breaking point. More often than not, that point is located somewhere near the middle of the mattress. That's how it happened to me.

As far as I'm concerned, females are God's most glorious creatures, and Lord knows, I've always been a sucker for a pretty face and a sweet smile. This time was no different. A few years ago, she took me by surprise, then took my heart completely. I fell hard.

It was too good to last. We split.

Then last year she showed up unexpectedly at my door. It was joyous. And of course, it was early fall, just cool enough to feel a stirring, a change, in the weather—and the heart. And that heart of mine, she worked it like a sculptor, shaping, stretching and molding it to suit her every whim and wish.

She was the master of the innocent peck on the cheek, the soft, gentle rub and the murmured mumble that might mean anything.

A few weeks after she arrived, the weather changed for good. Autumn deepened and the first hint of winter arrived. As the weather chilled, the action on my mattress heated up.

I was used to sleeping alone, and at first she respected my wishes. But when the frost hit the ground, she hit the bed.

It was innocent enough at first. No fooling around, just a sharing of space. But that soon changed. She became more demanding, snuggling tighter, smothering me with her constant closeness.

I tried to reason with her, saying it was too soon, that we really didn't need to do this now.

She insisted, working me in all those familiar ways. When the tender touch on the lips started, I knew I had to act.

"All right," I hollered. "You win. I'll do it."

I glared at her, jumped out of bed, plodded to the closet and began rummaging through the huge pile of junk on the floor. It had been a few years, but as soon as she spotted the object of her affection, her eyes almost popped out of their sockets.

When I dragged the electric blanket to the bed, my girl cat, Tammy, started howling like a fur-covered demon. "Yes, yes," she was saying, "the blanket. The electric blanket. That's it. That's what I want!"

She made so much noise her brother, George, wandered in to see what all the fuss was about. At the sight of the blanket, George was so stunned his eyes almost uncrossed.

I thought the electric blanket would solve my problem. It only made things more miserable. To begin with, once the blanket went on the bed, both cats decided it was their duty to stay there until spring's first robin arrived.

When I came home for lunch, did they dash to see me as before? Hardly. Aside from the occasional stroll to the food dish, they were glued to that bed. Even when I was in it. I didn't need a blanket. Forty odd pounds of close-by cat was enough to keep me sweltering through the last snowfall. Winter was a fur-filled horror. Summer was an all-too-short time of blessed solitude.

But summer is definitely over. You-know-what is back.

A couple of weeks ago, I felt it, that first real chill in the air...and in my bones. I came home for lunch unannounced and found Tammy scratching at the closet door. She looked at me expectantly and uttered a soft, guttural growl. Then she glanced up, and I swear, she winked.

It's gonna be a long, hot winter.

A Weighty Problem

"Hello. My name is Alex, and I have a problem."

It's an eating disorder. Actually, it's two. Their names are George and Tammy. They are my cats.

When they were babies, I nurtured them sweetly, always careful to keep the catnip fresh and the litter box empty. George and Tammy were sleek and slender youngsters, but as they aged, they seemed to grow a little bit faster—and a little bit bigger—than their pet peers.

I knew some breeds were naturally larger than others and thought nothing about it. They thrived and prospered until circumstances changed and they moved out for a while to live with some friends.

Recently, circumstances changed again and they moved back in. And now it looks like I may have to move out. Things are getting a little crowded at my place.

Simply put, George and Tammy are gaining weight at a speed that would make Oprah wince. And the problem isn't them...it's me.

When they moved back in, the gruesome twosome had a problem adjusting to their new surroundings. They were needy, nervous and edgy. I get the same way when I have a major life change like a new address or a heart bypass and knew how they felt. When I get a little out of sorts, I treat the problem with food. I tried the same thing with them.

They responded beautifully. Each time they heard the kibble crackle in the sack, their ears would perk up, their little voices would chirp and they'd groan with delight at each snack I sent their way. They were happy again, sunny and bright as a pair of new pennies.

At least while they were eating. As soon as the food was gone, so was their good mood. As the weeks passed, their attitude problems didn't disappear, just more of the carpet, each time they flopped on the floor.

With each added pound my concern grows, and it's reached the point where I'm afraid I'll come home one day and discover they've exploded like a pair of giant, fuzzy grenades.

And their impending explosion is having serious adverse affects on me. Especially when it comes to sleeping. The only way I can steal an afternoon nap is to bribe them to their bowls long enough for me to duck under the covers. I'm safe for about five minutes, at which time they walk away from their empty bowls and the subsequent shaking of the floor snaps me wide awake again.

At night it's even worse. As soon as I hit the sheets, they pounce on the bed and stare at me with eyes that say, "Feed me or suffer."

I do. And they eat. And then we do it all over again the next day. If Fox TV ever makes a special featuring the "World's Fattest Pets," George and Tammy will become major stars. Maybe they can hire an agent to send me postcards after I'm hauled off to pet jail for cat abuse.

So I'm asking for help.

And please, no diet suggestions. I tried cutting back on their food. Tammy expressed her displeasure by changing her litter box habits for the worse. George was a little more direct. Once he caught me walking through the room holding a Vienna sausage, and before I knew it, I was wearing George like a glove, trying to shake him off my arm as he gnawed ravenously at the scrap of meat.

I know exercise is good, and I could toss them outside to chase squirrels until they were slim and trim, but there are risks. Tammy might survive unless she's seduced by a Hollywood film crew looking for a fresh face to star in the remake of "The Blob," but George is another matter.

It's deer season. And considering his color and especially his size, George is probably safer inside.

Homeland Insecurity

A bird in the hand is worth two in the bush. A bird in the house is worth a column. Here it is...

The two cats stirred on the comforter as the alarm clock moaned in the darkness. When I hit the snooze alarm for the second time, they quit stirring and got serious. Tammy stuck a paw in my mouth, and George sat on my head.

I dragged myself out of bed, filled their bowls, showered and slipped off to work.

After a long morning, I headed home for lunch, hoping to snag a fifteen-minute power nap. Before I could doze off, I was startled by a rush of cool air across my face followed by an ominous *thump* on the floor next to the bed. I cracked an eye in time to feel a second breeze and to see what had caused it, which in this case was George, soaring across the bed like a fat, furry eagle in the direction of the kitchen.

Since their normal operating speed is slower than a waddle, I wondered what could have caused George and Tammy's airborne antics. Then the noises started. Cat owners know that while cats can produce many vocal sounds, they all mean one of two things, either "feed me" or "feed me NOW!"

But these sounds were unusual, strange primal growls and ear-splitting shrieks unlike anything I'd heard before.

I stumbled into the kitchen, where I immediately noticed the object of their none-too-friendly attention. It was a woodpecker, a short, fat bird with a big, long beak, flying from the kitchen window to the bathroom door and back again.

Without warning it turned and sailed past me toward the living room, the cats thundering behind in pursuit. It was only then I realized that the bird's fear at being trapped in a house and confronted by two cats the size of minivans was causing it some digestive distress.

The kitchen floor and countertop were spattered with bird droppings, as were the windows. And to my horror, so was my Roy Rogers bedspread, where Trigger had taken a hit to the hindquarters.

That spiteful act turned me from spectator to predator, and I followed the cats into the living room, determined to remove the dung-dropping monster from the house. The bird was bouncing from window to window, caroming off the couch and swooshing to the ceiling, pooping relentlessly all the while.

It flew back to the kitchen and I followed, stumbling over cats and dirty clothes. By then I knew the only solution was to drive the bird back to the living room, open the door and wait for it to fly away.

With a broom and a string of loud curses, I chased the bird back into the target zone. Then I yanked open the door and watched in horror as George dashed out onto the porch for the first time in his life.

I cornered him while he was still in shock, but then, as I hauled George back inside, Tammy shot out the door and screeched to a halt, horrified at the large vehicles roaring by 30 feet away. As I lugged her to safety, the long-beaked bird made its break and shot through the door, inches from my face.

I breathed a sigh of relief and skipped the Vienna sausage in favor of cold beer. After a minute or two the cats went back to sleep, and with twenty minutes left in the lunch hour, I decided to try and do the same.

I gazed down at the bed only to discover that Trigger hadn't been the only target in the bird's bombsight. Right there on my pillow sat another ugly reminder of the bird's visit. I dropped the pillowcase in the washing machine, burned the pillow and headed back to work.

On the way home, I bought a semiautomatic assault rifle and a woodpecker cookbook.

Next time that bird shows up...it's war.

The Great Flood

Since I'm the one with the dubious medical history, I figured that for the foreseeable future, most of my health care dollars would be spent on myself. My boy cat, George, has decided otherwise.

This unwelcome trend began a year ago when he busted a knee that left me with a hole in my wallet where the down payment for my long-awaited new car used to be.

Once the knee healed, I figured my problems were over. Once again, George decided otherwise.

I first suspected something was wrong when the alarm clock woke me up the other day. Usually, George does the honors. His technique is very effective. He starts with a gentle nudge to the face with his fat, fuzzy paw. If that doesn't work, he sits on my head. When 23 pounds of cat sits on your head, the choices are simply get up or risk wearing a neck brace to work.

But that morning the clock went off. George's sister, Tammy, was waiting as usual, but even after the kibble clattered into the bowls, George remained absent. I found him in the litter box. But he wasn't littering. He was squatting there with a serious look on his face but not producing any results. I made several trips home during the day to check on him. Each time I found him in the litter box, and each time, he was coming up dry.

At the end of the day, convinced he would explode if he didn't get relief, I went to the vet.

"He can't go," I explained. "Not making any water. Again."

The symptoms were the same as he had exhibited a few months earlier. That bout of bladder disorder was cured by a round of medication. I asked for a pill refill.

"No pills without another exam," I was told. "We have to be sure."

Early the next morning I dropped George off and told the doctors he had gone yet another night without getting his pump primed. I was told to check back after lunch, and did. They didn't have any test results because George still hadn't produced a urine sample to be tested. I was asked to come back later.

When I returned, a urine sample had been collected and I was told that yes, indeed, it was the same problem, and here are some pills and bring him back in ten days.

George doesn't like vet visits and was in a surly mood when I placed him in the car, hissing and snarling at imaginary enemies. As we drove home, I spoke gently to him and rubbed him between the ears. In a minute or so he quit hissing. Finally, his eyelids drooped to half-mast and he put on that dopey smile of his and I thought, good...he's finally happy.

Moments later I looked over again and discovered that what I took for a look of contentment was more like a look of relief.

I don't know the capacity of a cat's bladder, but George was in the process of emptying his. I could only sit and watch as 36 hours' worth of frustration (and urine) poured out in a blissful gush all over my cloth car seats. He finished as I reached the driveway.

When I let him in the house, he went straight to the litter box.

I went straight to the store and spent a small fortune buying cleaning products that promised to remove the most offensive odors from anything. I cleaned the car for an hour and went inside. George was not in the litter box. He was on my bed. Taking a nap.

I started to sit on his head, thought better of it and let him sleep. But when he woke up, I let him know in no uncertain terms that the next time he gets sick, I'm calling a cab.

Thrill from a Spill

Whoever said "Good things come in small packages" never spent Christmas with a cat. Or at least not with my two.

Where cats and Christmas are concerned, bigger is better. At least when it comes to packages. Anybody who thinks it's hard to entertain a cat just needs to empty a box or bag and leave it on the floor.

That's all it takes to send my bulbous babies, George and Tammy, into a frenzy. They'll check it out with the same care they would a snake, paw it a few times to make sure it can't fight back and then make their grand entrance.

How long they stay inside the box or bag depends on how jealous the other cat gets. Sometimes disputes arise and sometimes it gets ugly, but for cat entertainment, you can't top empty containers.

Or so I thought. But I recently discovered a new, even more exciting form of cat amusement.

I'm blessed with great pharmacists. Whenever I visit Lee-King Drugs, Bobby and Carol and John go to great pains to see I receive the finest farm-fresh medications. One of my favorites is aspirin, which I take every day. But recently I read something that indicated my daily dosage might be too high. I decided to cut back. The question was how much.

I didn't want to make such an important decision without expert medical advice, so I asked my druggist buddies for help. They recommended 81-milligram baby aspirin. I bought some. They were small and orange and much more stylish than the fat white ones.

I used my jazzy new pills for several weeks and was completely satisfied. Right up until what I call "The Aspirin Incident."

It was early. I was late for work. And not paying attention as I dumped the aspirin out of the bottle. I missed my hand. Aspirin went all over the floor. The cats were on the scene in seconds to see what goodies I had accidentally delivered.

Rather than shoo them away, I just watched. First, because I figured if they ate a baby aspirin, it wouldn't cause too much damage. Second, because my cats don't take pills. Period. I have the emergency room bills and scars to prove it.

They sniffed the pills and sauntered off. So did I, figuring to clean up the mess after work.

But when I came home, they were gone. Not the cats. The pills.

I panicked, thinking the critters had overcome their pill-o-phobia and accidentally OD'd on baby medication. Then I spotted an aspirin about five feet away from the site of the spill. I saw another lying in the next room. Two were wedged beneath the kitchen counter, and one had traveled down two stairs, around a corner and into the bathroom.

I finally figured it out. While I was at work, the cats had invented aspirin hockey.

I stationed myself quietly in another room. Over an hour passed and then, I heard it: a hiss, a low growl, the signal that the game was on. I stuck my head around the corner.

George and Tammy were facing off over a small orange puck. With ears back and tails up, they stared each other down like gunfighters. Then Tammy lunged at the aspirin and George countered and the pill went sailing. Both cats lumbered after it, slipping and sliding on the slick surface.

The battle raged under the bed, across the floor, and finally, into the closet, where the aspirin disappeared beneath a pile of dirty underwear. The cats looked at me and howled pitifully.

I dumped about five more baby aspirin on the floor. Then I picked up the dozen or so empty bags and boxes that had been on the floor since last Christmas.

They got a new game. I got my floor space back. Perfect.

When the Owner's Away, the Cats Will...

In the past, when I've had to be away for a day or two, one of my human kids was close enough to watch after my cats, George and Tammy.

This time, when the long weekend beckoned, the kids were not available. Since I didn't want to spend the money and time necessary to break in a new catkeeper, I took a deep breath, prayed briefly and decided to leave the cats..."Home Alone."

The plan had obvious flaws from the beginning. The first being cost. The fifty-pound bag of food (and matching amount of cat litter) was relatively cheap. It was the delivery systems that broke the bank.

For liquid refreshment I bought something that looked like an office water cooler and promised to dispense all the cool, clear water two cats could ever want. For food delivery, I chose a self-feeder that looked like a small plastic oil drum that squatted over a food dish. You fill the container with cat food, which spills into the bowl, and as the cats eat, gravity replaces the supply.

Since they normally eat from separate bowls, I bought two feeders to make them feel special. I decided to test the equipment before I left to make sure they had the hang of things.

The water cooler didn't interest them at all. The food dispensers were another story.

When I placed the new items on the floor, the cats looked at me, yawned and rolled their eyes as if to say, "What's Stupid doing?" But once I began to fill the containers, things changed in a hurry. Their eyes bulged and droplets of drool formed at the corners of their mouths as food gushed forth in a flood, overflowing the serving dishes with gobs of golden goodies. I imagine it was much the way they pictured cat paradise.

I dozed off to the sound of crunching kibbles. I woke up the next morning to the same sound, noticed the food supply had dropped drastically overnight, and refilled the containers as the cats staggered away to sleep off their feast.

They usually get agitated when I start to leave, so this time I packed quietly, snuck the bag out to the car and came back to tell them goodbye. They didn't even bother to get off the couch.

When I closed the door I heard a strange, unfamiliar sound. I thought it was a plaintive yowl of farewell.

Turns out it was probably more like...

"PARTY TIME!"

I'm still assessing the damage. It looks like they warmed up in the bathroom, which I had stupidly left wide open—with a full roll of toilet paper in the holder. It looked like a bomb had hit the Charmin factory.

Judging from the fact that the phone was off the hook (and on the floor), I assume they tried to call some friends to come over and join them. I had visions of sleazy cat parties with large quantities of catnip being ingested while everyone sat around grooming themselves and ignoring each other.

I'd left the computer off but not unplugged. They had managed to not only turn it on but rename a floppy disc to "(---{{{@#) and log on to AOL.

I expect a flood of unsolicited cat pornography in the coming weeks.

The remote control had been knocked to the floor, and the TV was on and running. It was turned to MTV, which served them right.

Took me half a day to clean up the mess, but the main thing is, the cats were all right. In fact, maybe a little too all right. When I woke up this morning, I saw a small brochure peeking out from under the couch. It was an ad for a four-day cut-rate cruise to the Bahamas. It had greasy paw prints all over it.

And when I picked it up and began to read, I swear I saw them grin.

Made in the USA
San Bernardino, CA
07 August 2017